OUR
UNION *WITH*
CHRIST

HARRISON HOUSE BOOKS BY DUANE SHERIFF

Identity Theft

OUR
UNION *WITH*
CHRIST

HOW YOU CAN ENJOY
A DEEP RELATIONSHIP WITH
THE LIVING GOD

DUANE SHERIFF

Published by Harrison House Publishers
Shippensburg, PA 17257

Cover design by Eileen Rockwell
Interior design by Terry Clifton

ISBN 13 TP: 978-1-68031-298-0
ISBN 13 eBook: 978-1-68031-299-7
ISBN 13 HC: 978-1-68031-301-7
ISBN 13 LP: 978-1-68031-300-0

For Worldwide Distribution, Printed in the U.S.A.
1 2 3 4 5 6 7 8 / 24 23 22 21 20

CONTENTS

INTRODUCTION

Our union with Christ is a great mystery waiting to be revealed. It's all about the miraculous sum total of our new identity in Christ as His bride, which affects just about everything. It affects how we believe and behave because all our actions (good or bad) come out of our "being" and who we believe we are. The union we have with Christ and our new condition as His bride affects how we view and approach life and its challenges. Our new condition in Christ is directly connected to our purpose in this life. We cannot fulfill that purpose if we do not know who we are. It truly takes a revelation from God to see our new condition in Christ. That's a radical statement, but it is the truth.

We are personally and specifically revealed in Scripture in a glorious and profound way. As we open our hearts, God delights in downloading spiritual knowledge, a clarity of His calling, and the power to fulfill that calling. He desires that we discover the exact gifting He has placed within each of us as well as the masterful principles He has laid out in Scripture for our success in navigating life. This includes our most intimate relationships, specifically *marriage*. I emphasize marriage because our relationship with Jesus is revealed and experienced in the biblical picture of matrimony. In this divine framework, the husband loves his wife as he loves himself and the wife receives the blessings of a loving, pursuing husband. God's amazing grace is displayed in Jesus as a magnanimous husband to us, the Church. It shows us that Jesus loves us as He loves Himself. He is nothing but a blessing to His bride. Our spiritual Husband asks for a simple response in faith—that as a "submissive," loving wife, we welcome Him with open arms, trust Him, and receive what He provides in His amazing grace.

The world and many religious traditions have distorted the true meaning of marriage. God desires to restore the original portrait, and thereby, restore our relationship with Jesus as His beloved bride. While this is *not* a book on marriage, God has chosen the biblical picture of marriage to reveal our relationship with Jesus and our new identity as His bride. Regardless of our marital status, marriage is a universal language that communicates God's unconditional covenant love for us the Church. In order to understand our relationship with our Husband Jesus, we must first understand marriage from God's perspective. This revelation of marriage as God ordained it connects us to our purpose in life as the bride of Jesus. Christianity is not about rules, regulations, and rituals but rather a beautiful love relationship with the Lord. Once we know who we are, we can clearly see what we have and can now do through Christ.

In my first book *Identity Theft,* we dealt with the identity crisis we were all born into through Adam and how we all labored under a fallen identity because of sin. In this book, we will discover how we now reign in life through the new birth and our new identity with Christ as His bride. Everything that was lost in the fall is now fully recovered in the resurrection of Jesus (our Husband).

CHAPTER 1

THE UNVEILING

Most everyone enjoys a good mystery. Whether it be a book or movie, the intrigue of discovering clues, developing hypotheses, and ultimately solving the case gives us a sense of adventure that keeps us hooked. Who doesn't enjoy a good Sherlock Holmes story that has been told and retold many times over the last century? Life is also full of mysteries waiting to be unlocked and explored as we grow and mature.

Sue and I have been married since 1980, and let me tell you, there are still *great* mysteries associated with the female and my wife that I am *diligently* (well, sometimes) trying to ferret out and identify. I don't know that I will ever totally figure out the right buttons to push but the adventure associated with working on it keeps me in hot pursuit of Sue in growing our relationship. It's the not knowing and excitement of figuring it out that creates a desire to keep seeking and stay on the quest for answers.

So it is with the Bible. There are mysteries associated with God and His Word that He desires to open up and reveal to us as we pray and search through the Scriptures. Too many believers get so discouraged on what they "don't know" in regard to God's will, plan, and purpose for their lives that they tend to lose sight of what they do know. The riches found in the mysteries of God are what make Christianity an adventure as we discover more and more of His abundant treasures. Let us never allow what we don't know to keep us from enjoying what we do know. This will encourage us to keep pursuing Him diligently, thereby daily unearthing the unknown mysteries of God. Mark 4:11 speaks of this: *"...Unto you it is given to know the mystery of the kingdom of God...."* Mind-bogglers such as the mystery of iniquity, the mystery of godliness, and many others, call us to the exciting pursuit of God and His personhood.

> Discovering and unlocking this mystery of our union in Christ will open a floodgate of encountering and enjoying God's love for us in a much greater way.

One of the greatest mysteries is the mystery of Christ in us. It is referred to as *the great mystery* and is the most colossal mystery of all. Discovering and unlocking this mystery of our union in Christ will open a floodgate of encountering and enjoying God's love for us in a much greater way. The apostle Paul speaks of this mystery in Ephesians 5:

> *For a man who loves his wife actually shows love for himself. No one hates his own body but feeds and cares for it, just as **Christ cares for the church**. And we are members of his body. As the Scriptures say, "A man*

*leaves his father and mother and is joined to his wife, and the two are united into one." **This is a great mystery**, but it is an **illustration of the way Christ and the church are one**. So again I say, each man must love his wife as he loves himself, and the wife must respect her husband* (Ephesians 5:28-33 NLT).

The apostle Paul lays out the beautiful picture of marriage in these scriptures as ordained by God—a loving partnership and mutual respect between a husband and wife. He goes on to make the startling statement that this union of man and woman is a great mystery that reveals the tremendous intimacy intended between Christ and His Church. The role and responsibility of a loving husband is a type and shadow of Christ; the role and responsibility of a submissive wife is that of the Church. God uses marriage as one of many pictures to help us see Him and receive His love. He longs to teach us our part in the relationship and show the purpose for uniting Himself to us.

> God uses marriage as one of many pictures to help us see Him and receive His love.

Paul also ties the marriage relationship of Adam and Eve in original creation to Jesus and the Church in the new creation. Ephesians 5:31 says *"...a man leaves his father and mother and is joined to his wife, and the two are united into one"* (NLT). This verse is a direct quote from Genesis 2:24, where Adam and Eve became one flesh. Just as Adam and Eve were no longer two, but one flesh in marriage, we, as the Church, are now flesh of Jesus' flesh and bone of His bone—no longer two but one spirit. When a couple marry, the parental cord is cut, and the authority and covering of father and mother no longer exist. There is the coming out from under the direct control of parents, leaving the parent-child bond and forming the husband-wife bond in the covenant of marriage. It's the leave-and-cleave moment.

In the same way, when we accept Jesus as Lord, the bond and friendship with the world is broken, and a new bond in our spirit man is formed with Jesus. Just like a man leaves his father and mother and is one flesh with his wife (in marriage), we leave the world and are joined to the Lord (in salvation). For years, I did not realize what it meant to become one with Jesus in my spirit when I accepted Him as Lord. I thought I was just supposed to try and live a better life *for* God instead of living a life in union and fellowship *with* God.

Paul continues this idea of our spirits united to Jesus in First Corinthians 6:15-17:

> *Don't you realize that your bodies are actually parts of Christ? Should a man take his body which is part of Christ, and join it to a prostitute? Never! And don't you realize that if a man joins himself to a prostitute, he becomes one body with her? For the scriptures say, "The two are united into one." But the person who is joined to the Lord is one spirit with him* (NLT).

The phrase "one spirit with the Lord" clearly implies that God wants a marriage-type relationship of intimacy with us that is personal, spiritual, and holy. This relationship contains all that Jesus brings to it, such as the armor of God for divine protection from our enemies and the authority of His name. In addition, we have the power of His indwelling Spirit and the revelation that we can do anything God calls us to do with the support and strength of Jesus as our Husband.

This truth is emphasized again in Ephesians where Jesus is declared to be above all things, and we are His body of which He is now the head. In the same way the husband is the head of his wife (see Ephesians 5:23), Jesus is now the head of His bride, the Church. *"...And gave Him to be the head over all things to the church, which is His body, the fullness of Him that filleth all in all"* (Ephesians 1:22-23).

We are as joined to the Lord in salvation and the new-birth experience as a man is joined to his wife in the covenant of marriage. I lived the first fifteen years of my Christian life totally and completely defeated because I did not know what happened to me at salvation. I had no idea of the change inside of me and my new identity connected to Jesus in a very real and powerful way in my spirit. I knew I was changed but had no clue that change meant I was united to Christ Himself.

SPIRITUAL MATRIMONY

The Church is described as the fullness of Him that fills all things. Few have really seen and boldly believed we are truly united to Christ in a spiritual marriage relationship. We have been joined to the Lord in spiritual matrimony in a very real way. It is this joining that Paul called a "great mystery."

Webster's number-one definition of mystery is "a religious truth that one can only know by revelation and cannot fully understand." In other words, a mystery is a divine secret hidden by God and revealed by the Holy Spirit. This is a marvel—something that is not common or earthly. It is both spiritual and powerful. This "great mystery" that Paul declared is the reality that we are united to Christ as husband and wife. When we are born anew, God *permeates* us in our spirit. We become "flesh of His flesh and bone of His bone." Within this mystery is the incredible love God has for us and the ability to enjoy our life in Christ.

THE MESSAGE OF SCRIPTURE (LOVE)

The real story of Scripture is God's love for us and all His creation. God is not angry with us and against us as so many have thought (and in some cases have been mis-taught). He truly is a good God and He is for us and not against us. Christ dying for us on the cross is God's expression of incredible love for the unlovely (Romans 5:8). Once I realized God's love for me in Jesus and His work on the cross, the Scriptures came alive and my life changed supernaturally. The love He has for us is one of the most amazing wonders of life, and yet, it is unknown by the masses. It is a great mystery to many today, one in which God delights and desires to reveal. All God has ever wanted from man, the apex of all creation, is to have a relationship founded on His epic love. God created us in His image and likeness to be containers and expressers of His kind of love. To receive His love for us and love each other.

> The real story of Scripture is God's love for us and all His creation.

In the past, I have often asked myself what I would do if I could ask Jesus a few questions face to face. Questions such as: What exactly is the theme of the Bible? What is the number-one commandment we have from God? What are Moses and all the Old Testament prophets trying to say? So really, what's the bottom line? While I may not see Him in the flesh to ask Him, Scripture reveals the answers.

> *"Teacher, which is the most important commandment in the law of Moses?" Jesus replied, "You must **love the LORD your God** with all your heart, all your soul, and all your mind. This is the first and greatest commandment. A second is equally important: '**Love your neighbor as yourself.**' The entire law and all the demands of the prophets are based on these two commandments"* (Matthew 22:36-40 NLT).

LOVING GOD AND PEOPLE

The entire message of Scripture is to love God and each other. That is so different than what I was raised to believe. These simple truths of loving God and people can't transpire until we know God loves *us!* John, the apostle of Love, declares that our love for each other (expressor) begins and ends with knowing God's love for us first (container). *"We love each other because He loved us first"* (1 John 4:19 NLT).

Once God's love is experienced and enjoyed, we are to love each other out of a "love debt" to God. Notice Paul's letter to the Christians in Rome in regard to debt:

"Owe nothing to anyone—except for your obligation to love one another. If you love your neighbor, you will fulfill the requirements of God's law. For the commandments say, "You must not commit adultery. You must not murder. You must not steal. You must not covet." These—and other such commandments—are summed up in this one commandment: "Love your neighbor as yourself." Love does no wrong to others, so love fulfills the requirements of God's law (Romans 13:8-10 NLT).

The entire message of Scripture is God's love for us, and thereby, our love for each other. To this day I am captured and overwhelmed by the unconditional, unmerited, un-occasioned love of God for me. It is truly an epic love story that we all need to hear. Galatians 5:6 states that *"... faith worketh by love."* When we see God's love by revelation, our faith soars.

HUSBAND AND WIFE ROLES

God created marriage and that special relationship of love to unveil His union with us in and through Christ. Pure Christianity has always been about relationship and not lifeless rules and regulations. Throughout this book, the Holy Spirit will be unveiling God's love for you and how God views you as His bride, the bride of Christ. As we approach our union with Christ in the context of marriage, we must think in terms of roles, not male or female. God doesn't see us as male or female, but rather as one spirit. In Christ, Jesus' role is that of our Husband, making our role as that of a wife—this has nothing to do with gender.

Wow! How amazing! What a mystery! A bride is precious and adored. She looks to her husband for support and protection. We are precious to Christ, and He desires that we search out the spiritual realities of our marriage to Him. Doing so will allow us to grow and to embrace Him in an ever-increasing way—even with affection and passion. He wants to expand our ability to fellowship with Him and to receive His goodness and blessings. Within our new identity as Christ's beloved, the extraordinary love of God is known and enjoyed. How do we position ourselves to receive the revelation of this great mystery? *"The secret of the Lord is with them that fear him; and he will shew them his covenant"* (Psalm 25:14). God doesn't tell everyone everything. His secrets are reserved for those who fear Him.

FEAR = REVERENCE AND RESPECT

To fear God is not to be afraid or scared of God but to reverence and worship Him with a fully committed heart. When we worship God with all our hearts, His secrets (mysteries) are revealed. In His love and compassion, God brings about a symbiotic union with Jesus that is to be enjoyed by all of His people. Believing what the Word says about this is essential because faith activates things in our spirit, which causes us to have the living experience and all the benefits of being loved by God and wed to Christ.

> Before the cross, divine secrets were hidden—not *from* us, but *for* us.

Before the cross, divine secrets were hidden—not *from* us, but *for* us. They were hidden from Satan and from those who would stand apart from God. They were kept safely until the time that

Jesus came and turned the world upside down by making a way for mankind to be free from the bondage of sin and death. It was specifically set up for when our hearts would be born again and would fear God with a reverential fear. It was set up for a heart that would serve and worship Him for His steadfast love and faithfulness.

The Scriptures say these are secrets that *"eye hath not seen nor ear heard,"* however look at what Paul says in First Corinthians 2, as he explains *whose* eyes haven't seen and *whose* ears haven't heard.

> *When I first came to you, dear brothers and sisters, I didn't use lofty words and impressive wisdom to tell you **God's secret plan**. For I decided that while I was with you I would forget everything except Jesus Christ, the one who was crucified. I came to you in weakness—timid and trembling. And my message and my preaching were very plain. Rather than using clever and persuasive speeches, I relied only on the power of the Holy Spirit. I did this so you would trust not in human wisdom but in the power of God. Yet when I am among mature believers, I do speak with words of wisdom, but not the kind of wisdom that belongs to this world or to the rulers of this world, who are soon forgotten. No, the wisdom we speak of is the **mystery of God**—His plan that **was previously hidden**, even though he made it for our ultimate glory before the world began. But the rulers of this world have not understood it; if they had, they would not have crucified our glorious Lord. That is what the Scriptures mean when they say, "No eye has seen, no ear has heard, and no mind has imagined*

*what God has prepared for those who love him." But it was to us that **God revealed these things by his spirit**. For his Spirit searches out everything and shows us **God's deep secrets** (1 Corinthians 2:1-10 NLT).*

In a rather straightforward way, Paul tells us that this classified information concerns the cross. The death of Jesus was an act of God's great love for us. It made a way for us to become new creations and gave us the ability to partake of a new life. Now, as believers, we have eyes to see and ears to hear if we choose to do so. We can clearly see and know the things of God and His good plan by the Holy Spirit of God.

All the new-creation realities—which are extravagant—are connected to Jesus and the phenomenal passion He exerted on the cross. That pivotal moment in history affects us in a very real and practical way. Jesus Christ is not casual or generic in the way He loves. He is not a long-distance lover or just a Facebook friend. Jesus laid down His life as our ultimate husband and hero. And through that, the most remarkable, intimate, and intense bond is made to a heavenly life—in the here and now and the hereafter.

> Jesus laid down His life as our ultimate husband and hero.

When we accept Jesus as Lord, we do not enter a casual, distant, or disconnected relationship. We are not helplessly, or in some cases, hopelessly struggling to get close to God or obtain something from Him. Notice again the apostle Paul's declaration of our union with Christ. *"For I have betrothed you to one husband, that I may present you as a chaste virgin to Christ"* (2 Corinthians 11:2 NKJV).

Jesus is our Husband, and we belong to Him in a very special and spiritual union. With His Spirit united to our spirit, we are engrafted to the Messiah Himself. Engrafting is the joining of two living things, and they begin functioning normally as one. When you engraft a branch to a vine, the life and power of the vine flows into the branch, bringing new life and fruit. The branch has no life or power of its own but receives from the vine. Jesus is the vine, and we are the branches engrafted (united as in marriage) to the Lord who is now our life. Notice how close Paul declares us to be with the Lord in Second Corinthians 5:17 (AMPC): *"Therefore, if any person is [engrafted] in Christ (the Messiah) he is a new creation (a new creature altogether); the old [previous moral and spiritual condition] has passed away. Behold, the fresh and new has come!"*

God, through His Holy Spirit, desires to unveil this engrafting to the Messiah. As we learn to fear the Lord (to worship and revere Him), the secrets of the Lord are being revealed. The deep things of God as they relate to His love for us are being uncovered as the eyes of our understanding are being progressively opened. *"But God has revealed them to us through His Spirit. For the Spirit searches all things, yes, the deep things of God"* (1 Corinthians 2:10 NKJV).

The things that eyes have not seen nor ears heard have been revealed by God's Spirit in our lives. It is a joy to realize that as we see and experience our heavenly connection, there is always more to see and know. Just as our relationship with the Lord is growing and we are maturing in Him, so is our revelation of the deeper things of God Himself.

Over the years that I have known the Lord, the Spirit has revealed to me many wonderful things that He has provided for us through His amazing grace and our simple faith. I have been overwhelmed by the realization of His desire to pour out blessings, and I have come to trust and rest in His zeal for our welfare. However, I didn't always feel this way. I was a negative thinker, raised around religious thinkers who didn't see God in the light Jesus revealed Him. God was often blamed or falsely accused for all the bad in our world, and in some cases, our lives.

When a couple's child dies, many will say things to try and comfort them that are not true and even slander the character of God. Things like "God needed another angel in heaven," implying God killed a child because He was short of angels in heaven. God's angel deficit in heaven was self-inflicted by removing angels from their original state due to their rebellion. Lucifer himself was cast down and out because iniquity was found in him. God is not killing our babies because He is hard up for angels. God is not doing bad things to any of us. He is not making us sick, poor, mean, or ugly for any cause. Jesus came to bring us life, and that in abundance, whereas Satan came to steal, kill, and destroy (see John 10:10).

Most of my younger life, I thought God was holding out on me. Or more to the point, I thought I just wasn't worthy of His favor. I simply felt like I couldn't do enough right or quit enough wrong to receive His love and blessings. My attitude was so bad that it actually took a lot of effort in applying myself and yielding to the Holy Spirit to renew my mind to the goodness of God and the abundance of His blessings and kindness. Even in my church attendance, I thought God was pleased to see others attend and then see me and go, "Oh no, you're here." That is so sad to think God would feel that way toward anyone seeking Him, but I did. I discovered He is unbelievably generous, and, at times, what the Word says about us just sounds too good to be true. However, it *is* true, and it will always *be* true. God loves us exceedingly and has blessed us enormously in Christ. God's epic love for us is unconditional, unmerited, and beyond human comprehension. You can't do enough good to get God to love you more or do enough bad to make Him love you less. God just loves you! Once the Holy Spirit unveils this, all we can do is worship and revere Him.

"NOD TO GOD" CROWD

Many Christians "nod to God," and they will say, "Yes, He loves me." There is a popular song, known by believers and unbelievers alike, "Jesus loves me, this I know...." But the truth is, most Christians don't pursue the reality of the richness of His love for us. God's love has to be taught and sought after, not earned or deserved, to be understood. We have to purposely take hold of it. How do we do that? We take hold through the Word of God and the

> You can't do enough good to get God to love you more or do enough bad to make Him love you less. God just loves you!

Spirit of God. The Holy Spirit is the only One who can reveal to us who we are in Christ. We are a new creation of God, an heir of the Kingdom and all that is within it, the *royal bride* of Christ, and *one spirit* with the Lord. All of these different facets of our identity can only be discovered in God's Word. Our feelings and circumstances cannot be indicators of this truth. It doesn't always look or feel like God loves us, but He does.

THE JOURNEY FROM HERE

I have so much to share. We will discover all the dimensions and aspects of marriage as God ordained it to be and the revelation of our union (marriage) to Jesus. We will look at the purpose of marriage as created by God and how it all relates to the Church, and we will consider how to bear fruit in the Kingdom. Believe it or not, that is all tied to our relationship with Jesus (the Word). We even explore supernatural change and how easy it is once you see Jesus and His glory. One of the chapters will even deal with God's love for us and what it actually looks like.

We have not even begun to imagine the spiritual dynamite that exists in our marriage to Jesus. What Jesus did on the cross in order to rescue His bride is "a marvel and mystery of a lifetime being unveiled." Don't let the mystery of how this whole thing works keep you from exploring the wonder of it in God's Word. Ask the Holy Spirit to guide your journey into the wonders of this pure and holy love.

> What Jesus did on the cross in order to rescue His bride is "a marvel and mystery of a lifetime being unveiled."

It is my confident conviction that all has been said in Jesus, all has been done in Jesus, and all has been given in Jesus. If that is true, and I believe it is so, then what is left to be said, done, or given? Jesus has done it all! All that is left is to declare it, receive it by faith, and celebrate this progressively wonderful relationship for the rest of eternity. Through our expanding discovery of Jesus' love and our kinship with Him, we receive the recovery of all good things that were lost in the fall. Jesus is God's final word to humanity, and He is more than enough for every need we have.

CHAPTER 2

OUR VICTORY

*You see, every child of God **overcomes** the world, for **our
faith is the victorious power** that triumphs over the
world. So who are the **world conquerors**, defeating its
power? Those who believe that Jesus is the Son of God.*
—1 John 5:4-5 TPT

Jesus is synonymous with victory. In taking our hand in matrimony, He makes *us* synonymous with victory as well—over sin, sickness, and the grave. We are victorious over lack and frustration, over confusion and doubt, over strife, and over every negative obstacle. Our simple faith brings us into a relationship with Jesus in which we now share, as a wife would, in all of His victory.

No enemy could withstand the power of Jesus' clandestine triumph on the cross. When it came to the crucifixion, even Satan was completely clueless. He walked right into God's plan. The rulers of darkness would never have moved upon the corrupted people of Jesus' day had they known the end result: their demise!

OUR UNION WITH CHRIST

> *Having **disarmed principalities** and powers, He made a public spectacle of them, **triumphing** over them in it* (Colossians 2:15 NKJV).

Jesus disarmed the powers of darkness and has called us to share in His victory. Instead of dealing with one man who went about destroying every dark work, Satan would now have to deal with the power of that one, sinless man, surging within multitudes—everywhere, all around the world. Jesus is now living in millions of people, and the Church multiplies the power of Jesus in a global expression. Satan became outnumbered and was defeated, because Jesus' death and resurrection was like tossing the seed head of a dandelion into the wind. Each tiny seed lands in the soil and they grow and send out more seeds that land and grow, until the whole field is overcome with dandelions. Had he known the great mystery, he would not have crucified Jesus. *"But the rulers of this world have not understood it; if they had, they would not have crucified our glorious Lord"* (1 Corinthians 2:8 NLT).

> Jesus disarmed the powers of darkness and has called us to share in His victory.

What a profound statement. The secular rulers of that day and those who were hostile in the synagogues did not understand how Jesus' death and resurrection would lead to a marriage relation with a global community—a body of believers who went about doing good and overcoming wickedness at every turn. First John 3:8 says: *"...For this purpose the son of God was manifested, that he might destroy the works of the devil."* When we discover who we are in Christ, we too—by God's Spirit—will destroy the works of the devil. In the book of John, Jesus tells us, *"Anyone who believes in me will do the same works I have done and even greater works, because I'm going to be with my Father"* (John 14:12 NLT).

In seeing and appropriating who we are *in, with,* and *through* Christ, we can now do all things, no matter the circumstance. The reason many do not believe in miracles today is they don't know we are united to Jesus. His very power as our Husband flows through us, His bride. Even from prison, Paul emphatically proclaimed: *"I can do all things through Christ who strengthens me"* (Philippians 4:13 NKJV). Notice he did not say he could do all things. We cannot do all things, but we can do all things through Christ. Only through our union with Christ are we able to see the supernatural things of God in our lives.

> The same Jesus who defeated the devil at every turn is now living in His Church causing us to always triumph in Jesus, our Husband.

Satan would not have crucified Jesus had he known the mystery of Christ in us who believe, the hope of all glory. The same Jesus who defeated the devil at every turn is now living in His Church causing us to always triumph in Jesus, our Husband. *"God always makes his grace visible in Christ, who includes us as partners of his endless triumph. Through our yielded lives he spreads the fragrance of the knowledge of God everywhere we go"* (2 Corinthians 2:14 TPT).

THE MYSTERY REVEALED

*...what we are setting forth is a wisdom of God, **once** **hidden** [from the human understanding] and now **revealed to us by God**— [that wisdom] which God devised and decreed before the ages for our glorifi- cation [**to lift us unto the glory of His presence**]* (1 Corinthians 2:7 AMPC).

God had a hidden plan completely for our benefit. It speaks of our active, supernatural alliance with Him. This was in God's heart before time as we know it. Satan knew the Messiah would come, but he had no idea that Jesus' sacrifice on the cross would include us—every single believer—past, present, and future— vicariously united with Him. Jesus brought an end to man's marriage to Adam (our old man, a sinner) and now brings a new marriage to Himself—a marriage in which our spirit is made the very righteousness of God (2 Corinthians 5:21, Romans 5:19). Satan, in his arrogance, did not see that Jesus would destroy the powers of darkness, destruction, and death, and in its place, create a new life in which believers have been made free!

Jesus—The Way, The Truth, and The Life—brings a vibrant, expansive existence for us. It is summed up in the image of a close, personal, and intimate marriage relationship with God. Jesus has betrothed Himself to us; He devotes Himself to us, and He has given us so much in the new creation. Our new condition is one of victor over Satan and darkness. We are no longer victims bound by chains of sin, but we are now victors bound to Jesus in righteousness.

The Passion Translation in First Corinthians 2:9-12 says it like this:

> *This is why the Scriptures say: Things never discovered or heard of before, things beyond our ability to imagine—these are the many things God has in store for all His lovers. But God now **unveils these profound realities** to us by the Spirit. Yes, He has **revealed to us** his inmost heart and **deepest mysteries** through the Holy Spirit, who constantly explores all things. After all, who can really see into a person's heart and know his hidden impulses except for that person's spirit? So it is with God. His thoughts and **secrets** are only fully understood by His Spirit. For we did not receive the spirit of this world system but the Spirit of God, so that we **might come to understand and experience all that grace has lavished upon us.***

God is revealing profound realities to us in regard to our new union with Christ. It is His Spirit who is sharing the deepest mysteries of the new creation joining with Christ and His Church.

REVEALING WHO WE ARE

In Matthew 16:13 Jesus ask the disciples, *"Who do men say that I, the Son of Man, am?"* (NKJV). After they gave a variety of all the wrong answers (John the Baptist, Elijah, Jeremiah, one of the prophets), Peter gave the correct answer: *"You are the Christ, the Son of the living God"* (Matthew 16:16 NKJV). Then Jesus made a profound statement: *"Blessed are you, Simon Bar-jona, for flesh and blood has not revealed this to you, but my Father which is in heaven"* (Matthew 16:17 NKJV).

Independent of the Spirit of God, man cannot know who Jesus is, why He came, and what His purpose was on the cross. It takes a revelation from God and that same Spirit to reveal to us who we are in Christ. No parent, philosopher, politician—or even a preacher—can fully reveal the great love Jesus has for us as His bride. God can use anointed men and women to teach, preach, and even write about it, but it takes a desire to have the Holy Spirit open the eyes of our understanding and download revelation of our exceptional position as Christ's bride, our new identity that is the source of our victory.

Paul said:

> *God has given me the responsibility of serving his church by proclaiming his entire message to you. This message was kept secret for centuries and generations past, but now it has been revealed to God's people. For God wanted them to know that the riches and glory of Christ are for you Gentiles, too. And this is the secret: Christ lives in you. This gives you assurance of sharing his glory* (Colossians 1:25-27 NLT).

Notice again how the message was hidden but now has been revealed to God's people. This secret, unveiled in our hearts, opens the door to all the riches and glory that God has secured in our Husband, Jesus. *Husband* is a strong, yet tender word. It is a word that He takes seriously. He is faithful and loyal regardless of our circumstances or any issues we face in life. He is committed to us in our covenant of marriage regardless of our actions. Simply put, He takes care of us.

PAUL'S TESTIMONY

Dear brothers and sisters, I want you to understand that the gospel message I preach is not based on mere human reasoning. **I received my message from no human source,** *and no one taught me. Instead, I received it by* **direct revelation from Jesus Christ.** *You know what I was like when I followed the Jewish religion—how I violently persecuted God's church. I did my best to destroy it. I was far ahead of my fellow Jews in my zeal for the traditions of my ancestors. But even before I was born, God chose me and called me by his marvelous grace.* **Then it pleased him to reveal his Son to me** *so that I would proclaim the Good News about Jesus to the Gentiles. When this happened, I did not rush out to consult with any human being. Nor did I go up to Jerusalem to consult with those who were apostles before I was. Instead, I went away in Arabia, and later I returned to the city of Damascus. Then three years later I went to Jerusalem to get to know Peter, and I stayed with him for fifteen days. The only other apostle I met at that time was James, the Lord's brother* (Galatians 1:11-19 NLT).

This secret, or great mystery of our union in Christ, did not come through any human. It was revealed directly to Paul by God Himself. In seeking the Lord, Paul got the clear image of Christ being fully alive inside of every believer. *"...It pleased him to reveal his Son to me...."* This ought to be encouraging to you—that God can and will communicate with you directly.

It was on the road to Damascus that the Lord confronted Saul of Tarsus and revealed our union with Christ. Saul thought he was persecuting believers (the Church) and discovered Jesus was united to His Church and took it personally like a husband would a wife. Acts 9:1-5 is where Saul's encounter with Jesus is shared.

> *Then Saul, still breathing threats and murder against the disciples of the Lord, went to the high priest and asked letters from him to the synagogues of Damascus, so that if he found any who were of the Way, whether men or women, he might bring them bound to Jerusalem. As he journeyed he came near Damascus, and suddenly a light shone around him from heaven. Then he fell to the ground and heard a voice saying to him, "Saul, Saul, **why are you persecuting me?**" And he said, "Who are You, Lord?" Then the Lord said, "I am **Jesus, whom you are persecuting.** It is hard for you to kick against the goads"* (NKJV).

"Why are you persecuting me?" "Who are you, Lord?" "I am Jesus whom, you are persecuting" (NKJV). Christ is so united to His Church that to touch or harm one of them is to do it to the Lord Himself! This must have come as a horrible shock and surprise to Saul. The people he was persecuting *belonged* to the crucified and resurrected Messiah, the One prophesied about!

During Jesus' ministry on the earth, Saul had been a student of Gamaliel (Acts 22:3), one of the leading Pharisees of that day. It is very possible that Saul had encountered Jesus in the flesh at some point during that time; however, on this particular day he encountered Him after the spirit. That is why he spent years in the Arabian desert processing this great mystery. He discovered it on the road to Damascus, but it took time with the Lord to process and then communicate it to the Gentiles.

I discovered my new identity with Christ in 1980 through an open vision. The vision drove me to the Scriptures where the Holy Spirit unveiled my new identity in Christ which is my divine connection to Him as my very life. I saw

> Christ is so united to His Church that to touch or harm one of them is to do it to the Lord Himself!

my union with Christ in His death, burial, resurrection, ascension, and seating in heavenly places. I've been on this journey and adventure in the full recovery of who I am in Christ, what I have and now can do through Christ, my Husband, for decades. We discover our union by revelation then recover in it through relationship with the Lord.

To this day, it pleases God to reveal Jesus to all of us in exactly the same way He enlightened Paul. In the Spirit, he saw the death of the old man in Adam (Saul the persecutor) and the birth of the new man in Christ (Paul the preacher). Even though Paul was one of the highest of the Pharisees and stringently obeyed every jot and tittle of the law, he saw that he was a sinful man. He saw the great mystery of how united Jesus is with His Church (Bride) and that as Christians we are "flesh of His flesh and bone of His bone" (Epheisans 5:30).

HOW TO PRAY

After he was converted, we read in Ephesians 1 how Paul prayed for us, the Church or bride of Christ. Sue and I pray this way for ourselves and others as well. He prayed:

> *That the God of our Lord Jesus Christ, the Father of glory, may give to you the spirit of wisdom and revelation in the knowledge of Him, the eyes of your understanding being enlightened; that you may know what is the hope of His calling, what are the riches of the glory of His inheritance in the saints, and what is the exceeding greatness of His power toward us who believe, according to the working of His mighty power which He worked in Christ when He raised Him from the dead...* (Ephesians 1:17-20 NKJV).

He is praying that we would by revelation understand and experience God's power in our lives and that we would know that we already have whatever we need as the wife of Jesus. Paul longed for us to realize the hope of our calling and to understand that the same power that raised Jesus from the dead is our inheritance. Simply put, His victory is ours!

God gives us access to the complete knowledge of His will, wisdom, and understanding. He does this through Scripture and through anointed preaching and teaching. God uses people, but He by the Holy Spirit is the true source of revelation. We can be confident that He wants us to receive that knowledge because His Word says He does. The Holy Spirit is ready and willing whenever you are. *"Ask, and it will be given to you; seek, and you will find;*

knock, and it will be opened to you. For everyone who asks receives, and he who seeks finds, and to him who knocks it will be opened" (Matthew 7:7-8 NKJV).

After praying for the saints, Paul requested prayer for himself in Ephesians 6:19-20. He asked them to pray like this *"...that utterance may be given me that I may open my mouth boldly to make known the mystery of the gospel...that in it I may speak boldly, as I ought to speak"* (NKJV). Paul knew that the right words would come from the very heart of God. He desired to be so empowered to clearly speak what God intended to be made known to His people. He wanted to speak about this seemingly wild condition—being betrothed to Jesus—without intimidation. Rather with great boldness, Paul wanted every heart to light up with the divine realization that Christ exists tangibly in us and relates to us as a loving husband rather than an intimidating master. He sees us as a partner in eternal life, versus a servant that is here only to wait on and obey the "boss." He knew it would take the Holy Spirit working in and through him to change people's lives.

Jesus in His final words to His disciples in John 16 is preparing them for His departure. He makes a statement that was very difficult for them to understand at the time, sbut later would be clear and life changing: *"But in fact, it is best for you that I go away, because if I don't, the Advocate won't come. If I do go away, then I will send him to you"* (John 16:7 NLT).

They had seen Him walk on water, raise the dead, cleanse lepers, and feed thousands with a little boy's lunch. So how could it be better for Him to no longer be with them? The Holy Spirit coming and being in them and with them was better than Jesus being with them in His physical body. Jesus had many things to say but the disciples could not understand because they were not born again or Spirit filled. Today, Jesus is not limited to one body in one physical place, but as I stated earlier, His body is now a global body made up of millions of believers. That actually is a benefit and better than Him being in one physical body today, limited to one geographical region. He went on to explain and say to them: *"There is so much more I want to tell you, but you can't bear it now. When the Spirit of truth comes, he will guide you into all truth. He will not speak on his own but will tell you what he has heard. He will. He will bring me glory by telling you whatever he receives from me. All that belongs to the Father is mine; this is why I said, 'The Spirit will tell you whatever he receives from me'"* (John 16:12-15 NLT).

Jesus had to leave so that the Holy Spirit could come. Now that we are born again and a new creation in Christ, the Holy Spirit can guide us into the truth of who we are and what we have and can now do in Christ. The disciples had not yet experienced the new creation because that didn't happen till the death, burial, and resurrection of Jesus. The "things to come" that Jesus was referring to were the new-creation realities—the new promises and blessing that are being revealed by the Holy Spirit. Jesus in union with His Church as a husband is to his wife is the mystery the Holy Spirit is unveiling. Before they were born again and Spirit filled, the disciples could not understand this great mystery.

A LOVE STORY

God's Word is the ultimate love story between God and man—all the way from Genesis to Revelation. From the beginning, we see His unconditional dedication to Adam and Eve, even after they had sinned and broken His word. Despite the consequences of their sin, God promised there would be a Rescuer. There would be One who would come through the seed of a woman, who would crush the serpent's head, who would bring life in the place of death, and who would bring us back to Himself. He had already arranged for man's separation from his Creator to be perfectly repaired, so that they could again be in a close relationship and walk together in the cool of the day. All along, a fix-it plan was in place. All along, God's relentless pursuit of man has been for good, not evil. His regard for us is seen throughout Scripture, and the grand finale is displayed in Revelation 21:1-3:

> *Then I saw a new heaven and a new earth, for the old heaven and the old earth had disappeared. And the sea was also gone. And I saw the **holy city**, the **new Jerusalem**, coming down from God out of heaven like a **bride** beautifully dressed for her **husband**. I heard a loud shout from the throne, saying, "Look, God's home is now among his people! **He will live with them**, and they will be his people. God himself will be with them"* (NLT).

The gathering of the bride of Christ is the lofty notes of an eternal symphony. The symphony reaches its crescendo as the bride is prepared and adorned for her husband. His bride, a city of His people, makes her entry as the New Jerusalem. She is the Church that has prepared herself for her bridegroom. She is the temple of God because Christ lives in her and rules and reigns

> The gathering of the bride of Christ is the lofty notes of an eternal symphony.

as a loving Husband who hovers over his wife and rejoices in her presence. And just as a husband and wife mature and grow in their relationship to one another, we will forever continue to grow in our relationship with Jesus.

As we pursue further understanding of the great mystery of our union with Jesus, it is my sincere hope that you will allow the Holy Spirit to reveal to you the perfect work of Christ on the cross. That together, we may fully understand our new identification with Christ and the magnitude of our life as being one spirit with Him, unveiled in the splendor of marriage. We have entered into a marriage relationship where Jesus is our victory. Everything He is and did was for us, His bride. Everything we are, can do, and can have is because we married into it. We don't deserve it, and we cannot earn it. All we need to do is simply enjoy it by faith because of Jesus.

CHAPTER 3

HONOR MARRIAGE

*Let marriage be held in **honor** (esteemed worthy, precious, of great price, and especially dear) in all things. And thus let the marriage bed be undefiled (kept undishonored); for God will judge and punish the unchaste [all guilty of sexual vice] and adulterous.*
—Hebrews 13:4 AMPC

As it was originally designed, marriage brings male and female together in a union that links them physically, mentally, emotionally, and spiritually in a profound way. Both parties are changed and strengthened because of it. God obviously takes marriage very seriously, and we should do no less. It certainly should not be entered into or exited out of lightly. God desires for us to value and highly respect this institution and our various positions within it. We don't see that kind of attitude very much in today's culture, but within the Church, we ought to see marriage as sacred, a reflection of God's commitment and gift to us.

I realize this analogy can be tough to swallow because many marriages are carnal, fragmented, subject to strife, upset, frustrated, critical, and on the brink of divorce. But when I speak of marriage being a reflection of God's love for us and actually a highly valuable legacy, I'm referring to the God-kind of marriage, which all believers ought to strive to learn about and achieve. At least you can understand that, as it is described in Scripture, we can be thankful for marriage and a blessing to be held in high esteem. It's not called Holy Matrimony by accident.

> God obviously takes marriage very seriously, and we should do no less.

When I entered into a marriage covenant with Sue, I was uneducated and uninformed about my role as a husband and her role as a wife. I certainly did not understand that marriage was a union referring to Christ and the Church. I knew I loved her on a very basic level, but I was immature in many areas of my life. I believe God brought us together, but it takes more than just a knowledge of God's will to build a healthy marriage. I knew I had a long way to go, and boy, was I open and eager to learn!

THE DREAM HONEYMOON—NOT!

In 1980, I was a broke college kid barely surviving. Even mac-n-cheese was stretching my budget and Ramen noodles had not come out on the market. During that time, I fell in love with the most beautiful woman named Sue. We were married in a simple and cheap wedding ceremony in a friend's home. At the time, we were both living in Orlando, Florida, so we decided to spend our honeymoon one hour away at Daytona Beach. Because of the generosity of some friends of ours, we were able to spend four days in a room that overlooked the beach.

On the day of our wedding, I had a bright idea. I wanted to surprise Sue by fixing up our honeymoon suite. I went to that small double room and laid out flowers and candles. The hotel discovered that we would be on our honeymoon, so they supplied a small bottle of champagne and two glasses. I put it on ice in one of my tennis ball stands. I just kept thinking, *WOW! How awesome is this? A room that overlooks Daytona Beach? What could go wrong?*

Some of you may be thinking, *Awww... how sweet was that?!* But hold on, you might very well change that assessment because on my way back to get ready, I had a flat tire. *Really!* It was not good folks! I then had to fix a flat tire on my truck, get back, get cleaned up and dressed in my suit before the wedding started.

Remember, this was before cell phones were available to a person of my economic status, so I had no way to contact Sue or anyone else to let them know of my plight. Needless to say, they were all a little bit on edge, but I got there with a whole *three* minutes to spare! And, thank goodness, for a late-evening wedding and dim lights because no one even noticed that I'd borrowed my father-in-law's tie; mine had gone missing in the chaos! That's a great way to start a marriage, right? Praise God for His mercy and the mercy of Sue and her family. She still married me, and soon we were off to the beach (well, after we cleaned all of the newspapers out of my truck, which had been lovingly stuffed in there by some well-intentioned friends)!

It was quite late by the time we got on the road, and all that either of us had eaten that day was one piece of wedding cake that we smeared in each other's faces. The only thing open by that time was a Waffle House, filled with smoke, sleep-deprived truck drivers, and drunks trying to sober up before going home. It looked like the famous bar scene right out of Star Wars. I didn't care, though. I was proud of my beautiful bride and paraded her in, ink-smudged wedding gown and all! We definitely got some stares, sneers and rude remarks, but we didn't care. We ate and got back on the road.

Once we got to our room, we decided to open the champagne and try some. After all, it was free, and we were very naive. Let me just say that it was the foulest-tasting stuff we had ever had! We set the glasses down on the end table beside the bed and had the most wonderful night...until about three in the morning when I sat straight up and began yelling, "Fire! Fire! There's a fire!" I grabbed the glasses of champagne and proceeded to douse myself and Sue with that awful substance. And then...I woke up! I was so embarrassed—I had been dreaming. I was convinced that my sweet little wife must have thought that she had married a crazy person. However, after laughing hysterically for a few minutes, Sue simply got up, put on some dry clothes, and moved to the other bed. She even let me get out of that wet, sticky mess and join her.

The next day we began getting ready for a romantic stroll on the beach when we were informed that acid rain was falling, and we were confined to our room until it quit. The honeymoon was not too bad for me, but it was not quite the fairy-tale honeymoon Sue had dreamed of for so long! To this day, I don't know if acid rain was a real thing or a hoax, but it certainly worked out well for me at the time!

SEEKING HIS WILL

We had a pretty rough start, but we knew we could do well together. We both decided to seek God's will for our lives, so we could discover what this whole "I do" business was supposed look like. I wanted to be the husband God wanted me to be, and Sue longed to be the wife God called her to be. Together, we were determined to have a marriage that would be pleasing to God, a blessing to each other, and one that would survive all of the winds of adversity that would surely come to try and separate us. We wanted God's perspective and His truth regarding who had what responsibilities in our new found life as Mr. and Mrs. We quickly discovered that much of the traditional images of marriage had not been accurate. Many of the images of our union to Jesus have not been accurate either.

The Word tells us that husbands are to love their wives as they love themselves. They are to honor, protect, and provide—not abuse, control, or manipulate. While wives are to be submissive, they are not to be walked on. They are meant to be helpmeets, (not help mats) partnered with and lifted up. God's Word also says that the husband and wife are to "submit one to another in the fear—the respect—of the Lord" (Ephesians 5:21).

In the world at large, marriage has become an outdated and antiquated idea, a "not for us cool people" concept. Some say it had its place in pre-dinosaur days and is simply irrelevant to this new age of so-called enlightened and progressive thinking. The world has been on a path of destroying and redefining the God-ordained purpose of marriage for many years. This path seems right to man, but the end of it is death to the family and to a morally good culture. In the way that the teaching is handed down through the generations, it will ultimately undermine our children's development and preparation for life and then their children after them.

God is a generational God. He is the God of Abraham, Isaac, and Jacob. Believe it or not, God's plan for man is marriage, families, and generational blessings. With few exceptions (a call and gifting to be single), we were created to live life in companionship and fellowship with a mate. I don't mean to say that it is wrong if, as an adult, you are not married. There is a time and season for everything. And some of us, like the apostle Paul, are called to be single, but that call is for the gospel's sake and a gift of celibacy accompanies it (see 1 Corinthians 7). Being single and sexually active or "burning with lust" is not God's will. There is just no getting around it; the backbone of every civilized society is the family unit. It was created by God as husband and wife and dad and mom. His plan was for children to have parents who will nurture and train them in social skills and the basics of right and wrong as well as leaving a legacy of faith.

> The world has been on a path of destroying and redefining the God-ordained purpose of marriage for many years.

Please know, I am not naïve, and the pushback on traditional marriage as well as the confusion regarding the roles of husband and wife do not surprise me at all. To be completely honest with you, I've had my own issues with specific roles in marriages and what God's idea and purpose of marriage looks like. The Archie and Edith Bunker *All in the Family* (Millennial Alert! You may have to Google this one) image of marriage was never God's image. I will admit that the Church is often misinformed, or in some cases uninformed, on the biblical perspective of a spouse's role. I recognize that there are abuses, control issues, a lack of loyalty, and, sadly, a lack of commitment that too often makes divorce appear to be the best and easiest option, but the problem really lies with a gross misunderstanding of the nature of marriage.

> There is just no getting around it; the backbone of every civilized society is the family unit.

Most modern marriages begin on the basis of romance or physical desire. The hope that having a mate will "complete" us and keep loneliness at bay plagues our society. Can I be bold enough to go so far as to say that marriage sometimes represents a way to escape financial or emotional problems or a way to "find happiness"? All of these are commonly held beliefs that are wrong but held by many believers. Due to these and many other misconceptions, the ideas of how a husband and wife are to relate in the marriage relationship is ambiguous at best.

THE BIG SURVEY

Years ago, as a young pastor, I did a survey in the church. I went to a number of people and asked them, "Why did you get married?" The answers were amazing to me. In many cases, no one could offer any answer at all. Regrettably, in some cases, I created doubt in people's minds. Some responded with "Yeah, why *did* I get married?" I wasn't intending to create marital problems and commitment issues; I was only hoping to gain some knowledge for myself concerning marriage in general. The only knowledge I gained was that many Christians were as confused as I was when I first got married.

I believe God desires to change all of that. None of us should enter marriage without a basic understanding of what we are doing. We need a knowledge of marriage and that knowledge needs to come from God and His Word. Look at the apostle Peter's view of marriage:

> *In the same way you married men should live consid-erately with [your wives], with an intelligent recogni-tion [of the marriage relation], honoring the woman as [physically] the weaker, but [realizing that you] are joint heirs of the grace [God's unmerited favor] of life, in order that your prayers may not be hindered and cut off. [Otherwise you cannot pray effectively]* (1 Peter 3:7 AMPC).

God wants to teach us to have an intelligent recognition of the marriage relationship. In Oklahoma talk, that means use your brain when it comes to your spouse and be considerate, realiz-ing we are heirs together in the grace of life. We have both been equally loved and blessed by Jesus. In this life as members together of God's Kingdom, we all have the same Holy Spirit, the same name of Jesus, and the same power and authority available to each of us. We have the same access to God and His throne with no sense of inferiority as male and female. Jesus and His Kingdom have brought about a true equality between the races, genders, eco-nomic status, as well as our backgrounds. Husbands and wives are heirs together in the grace of God. *"There is neither Jew nor Greek, there is neither slave nor free, there is neither male nor female; for you are all one in Christ Jesus"* (Galatians 3:28 NKJV).

There is to be a mutual respect in the relationship. Our prayers and their ability to effect change are connected to our intelligent recognition of our marriage to Jesus. God wants us to understand our new identity and dwell in harmony with our Husband Jesus. We are joint heirs with Jesus and are ruling and reigning together in this life. Jesus knows us as the weaker vessel but also as heirs together in the Kingdom of God. Our partnership as husband and wife brings powerful change in this world. If we dishonor one another in our natural marriages, our prayers are hindered. That means marriage is spiritual, not just natural. How we dwell together is connected to our spiri-

> Can you imagine the looks I get when people ask me why their prayers are unanswered, and my response is, "Let's look at your marriage"? Who thinks like that? God does.

tual life. Can you imagine the looks I get when people ask me why their prayers are unanswered, and my response is, "Let's look at your marriage"? Who thinks like that? God does.

Jesus and I are co-laborers together in the Kingdom. I've not always kept up my end of the deal, nor have I been the best wife in the world to Him. I'm so excited that Jesus will never leave or forsake me. I'm learning to dwell together with Jesus with an intelligent recognition of our union together. Jesus is the grace element in our partnership, and you and I are the faith element. Jesus has abounded toward us in grace, and we are yielding and receiving all His benefits by simple faith. Jesus and His name carry the power over all obstacles in this life. While Jesus has the power, we, as His wife, have the authority. This has been God's plan and purpose since the creation of man: God and us working together, ruling and reigning over all of creation.

CHAPTER 4

WHO CREATED MARRIAGE?

To everything there is a season, a time
*for every **purpose** under heaven.*
—Ecclesiastes 3:1 NKJV

Everything and everyone have a purpose. Marriage is no different, and yet most people have never even thought to consider the purpose, thereby diminishing the experience of being happily married. The purpose of marriage must be understood or there will be an abuse of it, and ultimately, the frustration of its original intent. The purpose of a thing is always found in the creator of that thing, not the creation itself. A car doesn't know its purpose, the manufacturer does (Ford or Chevy, etc.). That's why every car comes with an owner's manual. That manual was designed by the creator of the car.

GOD'S IDEA

Marriage is a construction of our creator God. He has the manual explaining the purpose and how it works. If we take marriage out of its original design, we create a distortion, and we become just as confused as many in our world are today. We have forgotten the purpose of marriage, and in some circles, we have completely forgotten what marriage actually is. No wonder so many marriages end in deep hurt and brokenness. If we don't know what a marriage is, who created it and to what end, how can we be happily and successfully married or reflect Christ and the Church?

This is why so many have a distorted picture of Christianity. Just like people are confused over marriage, people are equally confused on what it means to be saved, born again, and married to Jesus! Why did Jesus unite His Spirit to our spirits as believers in holy matrimony? It wasn't just so we could go to heaven but live a totally defeated life here on earth. Not at all!

Just like the revelation of the purpose of my marriage to Sue has produced a fruitful and beautiful life together; revelation of my marriage to Jesus has produced a fruitful and beautiful life together changing others for the glory of God. I knew it was right and God's will for me to marry Sue, but as far as what God actually thought about marriage, I was oblivious. Although Sue knew more than I did, we were both hungry for more understanding. We had so many questions. And as you already may have heard, inquiring minds want to know!

Who created marriage? Adam and Eve? Government? An individual? Israel? The President...? The Supreme Court? What is a marriage supposed to be like and who gets to say so? What is the biblical idea of a husband and wife relationship? Does it really matter? Does God even care about marriage anymore? What is submission in marriage? Do children really need a dad and mom? Why is divorce so bad? Are men and women really the same kind of people as my college professors asserted? A marriage license is just a piece of paper, so what's the big deal? These were all important questions, and we set out to find the answers.

WHO CREATED MARRIAGE?

To settle these questions, we studied the Scriptures— the unshakable Word. Jesus is the Word of God made flesh. He is called *The Living Word,* because He embodies the written Word, which is infused with the quickening of His life and is designed to infuse us with that same life, wisdom, and understanding. Jesus is, if you will, the Bible with eyeballs and hands and feet. What He says is rock-solid truth, no matter what. If we want to know *truth,* we must go to The Way, *The Truth,* and The Life. That is the source for everything concerning marriage. God's Word is where we find truth despite a world filled with falsehoods, distortions, and lies. Jesus prayed this way, *"Make them holy by your truth; teach them your word, which is truth"* (John 17:17 NLT). He also said to believers, *"You are truly my disciples if you remain faithful to my teachings. And you will know the truth and the truth will set you free"* (John 8:31-32 NLT).

If we can know what Jesus says about marriage, then we'll know the truth that will bring freedom and revelation. When the people of Israel asked Jesus a question regarding marriage, Jesus referred back to original creation, affirming who the Creator of the institution of marriage is. The book of Mark records how Jesus answered the Jew's question about why Moses allowed them to get divorces. *"But Jesus responded, 'He wrote this commandment only as a concession to your hard hearts. But 'God made them male and female' from the beginning of creation. "This explains why a man leaves his father and mother and is joined to his wife, and the two are united into one." Since they are no longer two but one, let no one split apart what God has joined together"* (Mark 10:5-9 NLT).

Jesus went all the way back to original creation to apply what God said to Adam and Eve about their union and how it was intended to be that way even these thousands of years later. Jesus' words still bear witness to God's plan for marriage from the beginning. If God joined them together, then God has joined Sue and I together, as well as you and your spouse. Marriage was created by God before government, Israel as a nation, the Church, or presidents or supreme courts. Marriage is the oldest institution known to man and was here before sin entered the world. That's how special and holy it really is.

> If we can know what Jesus says about marriage, then we'll know the truth that will bring freedom and revelation.

GENDER ASSIGNMENT

Jesus said that God made them male and female intentionally (Mark 10:6). He is the Author and Creator of our gender. Our gender assignment was established in our mother's womb, independent of our feelings or social pressure to re-assign us. Gender is not about "choice." Psalm 139:13 in the New Living Translation says, *"You made all the delicate, inner parts of my body and knit me together in my mother's womb."* Genesis 1:27 says, *"God created man in His own image; in the image of God He created him; male and female He created them."* He makes us male or female. *He* formed us exactly as it pleased Him as creatures who worship Him along with all of creation. To resist our gender assignment as male or female is rebelling against the Creator God. When we worship creation instead of our Creator, we throw things into chaos (Romans 1:25). When we worship Creator God rather than anything He has created, we come into divine order, releasing the flow of divine blessing.

MALE AND FEMALE—GOD'S DESIGN

Jesus said that God joins us together in marriage as male and female (see Mark 10:6). It's a God thing, not a man thing. God made us male and female from the beginning, and our design as male and female was for marriage. Moses recorded God's plan for man from the beginning.

> *Then God said, "Let us make man in Our image, according to Our likeness; let them have dominion over the fish of the sea, over the birds of the air, and over the cattle, over all the earth and over every creeping thing that creeps on the earth." So God created man in His own image; in the image of God He created him;* ***male and female He created them*** *(Genesis 1:26-27 NKJV)*
>
> *Therefore, a man shall leave his father and mother and be joined to his wife, and they shall become one flesh. And they were both naked, the* ***man and his wife,*** *and were not ashamed (Genesis 2:24-25 NKJV).*

When we combine what Jesus said in Mark 10 with what Moses recorded in Genesis 1 and 2, we see God's plan for man.

Jesus and Moses both declared that "man"—meaning all of mankind, both male and female—has been given authority and dominion over all creation. Though there are different callings, capacities, and measures of authority for everyone, both genders are equal in value in their bearing of God's image and in exercising their authority. Men and women are equally loved by God, and both are bestowed with the same inheritance in Jesus. They are equally blessed, with the same promises and provisions in Christ. However, men and women are not the same, much less interchangeable.

> Men and women are equally loved by God, and both are bestowed with the same inheritance in Jesus.

The moment God created Eve and brought her to Adam, as male and female, they didn't have any problem understanding the blueprint for marriage, nor did they have any trouble understanding God when He said, "Be fruitful and multiply." He designed their coming together in marriage. There was a unity in their diversity that made them one flesh and caused them to bear fruit. There was no divine unity in sameness. We can be certain that God knows the roles and responsibilities. He also knows the purpose of marriage. All of it still applies to us today. We need to remember that every marriage, contains a dynamic that Paul referred to as a great mystery. Marriage is something natural that unveils something supernatural; marriage, therefore, is holy, and spiritual.

ORIGINAL MARRIAGE BLUEPRINT

*And the Lord God said, "It is not good that the man should be **alone**; I will make him a **help meet** for him* (Genesis 2:18).

This is where the institution of marriage and its purpose begins to unfold. Notice Adam (man) didn't come up with the original idea. He didn't go to God and say, "Hey, get me a woman; I'm lonely down here." No, Adam was doing just fine: he could hunt and fish without any nagging or complaining about how he wasn't home enough (Just kidding...let it go!). Notice again: God approached Adam (man), Adam did not approach God. God came up with the idea. He created marriage so the Creator gets to define the creation however He wants. If it was man's creation, then man could define it or even re-define as many times as he wanted. If government, the Supreme Court, or other officials were the creators of the institution of marriage, then they would have the authority to change the definition. God gave man authority over the birds, fish, cattle, and earth; but He did not give man the authority to create or define marriage. God gives a president authority to rule and lead in civil, domestic affairs, but not spiritual matters.

> Marriage is something natural that unveils something supernatural; marriage, therefore, is holy, and spiritual.

CORRECT IMAGE OF MARRIAGE

Society at large has a very poor impression of marriage, as if it is just about "expressing" your feelings and warding off loneliness. There *is* a piece to marriage that has to do with not being alone, but not in the way the world imagines it. Many regard "alone" and "loneliness" as the same thing. They simply are not. In some cases, that flawed concept has weakened marriage and the relationship between husband and wife.

Adam was alone, but he was not lonely. There is a difference between the two. Alone is an external condition; lonely is internal. I have been alone and able to experience God's love and presence in my heart and life whether I was in the woods, at home studying, or working on a book. On the other hand, I have also been in the middle of a crowd and felt very lonely. In the midst of all sorts of people, I've experienced feelings of rejection or a sense that I really didn't fit in or belong. With Adam, there was none of that. He simply was alone.

With that said, in the beginning, after God created different things on different days, He said, "It is good." At the end of six days of creation, He stepped back and said, "It is very good" (see Genesis 1:31). But in Genesis 2, God said there was one thing that was not good—a bachelor. Basically, He told Adam, "You need a friend, a companion of your own kind, a partner in life." In Genesis 2:18, we find one of God's intended purposes for marriage.

Again, marriage is God's plan for man with few exceptions. We were not intended to live life alone. How does any of this point to Christ and the Church? If the first marriage in Scripture points to Christ and the Church, then Adam was a type of Christ and

Eve the Church. Jesus was not lonely as the second man—the last Adam—but He was alone. The Church is a "helpmeet" to Jesus— co-laborers together in the grace of life. Through the new birth, we have a partnership with Jesus that makes us one of His own kind, and yet, we are still different. Just like man didn't initiate or create marriage, the new creation in Christ (see 2 Corinthians 5:17) was God's idea not man's idea. We are not saved by the will of man but by the will of God (see John 1:13). God never intended for Adam to rule and reign over creation alone, nor does God will for Jesus to rule and reign alone in the new creation; that is where we come in!

> God never intended for Adam to rule and reign over creation alone, nor does God will for Jesus to rule and reign alone in the new creation; that is where we come in!

In our marriage union with Christ, we are now a blessing to Jesus in the earth. We are here to represent Him as His ambassador (see 2 Corinthians 5:20). We are heirs together of the grace of life, and He as our husband has all power in heaven and earth. We as His wife have been given authority in His name. With His power and our authority, we are ruling and reigning together as husband and wife in this life.

CHAPTER 5

WHY GET MARRIED?

Let's get back to that survey I did years ago on marriage and why we get married. This survey was not just about natural marriage.

I really wanted to discover if being confused on why we enter marriage affects our reasoning on why we got saved and married to Jesus? Could it be that if we don't know the reason for marriage in the flesh, we are confused on our spiritual marriage to Jesus?

> Could it be that if we don't know the reason for marriage in the flesh, we are confused on our spiritual marriage to Jesus?

When I did my survey, I asked the question, "Why did you get married?" Unfortunately, all of the answers I received actually addressed reasons to *not* get married!

Here are the top five:

ANSWER #1—"TO BE HAPPY." (*WRONG ANSWER!*)

How's that working out for you? Even though God longs for us to be happily married, we should not get married to be happy. Happiness can never be found in people, places, or things. When we look to these, we set ourselves up for disappointment and heartache. Think of tuning into your favorite radio station for music to make you happy on a road trip. We quickly begin to lose the signal the further down the road we travel. In time whatever or whoever we tune into for our happiness, life will begin to quickly take us away from that signal. The things and people we look to for our happiness can actually lead to unhappiness. While God wills to make our spouse a blessing to us, only God can bring true happiness. Consider the following truth: "*Where there is no vision (no revelation of God and His word) the people are unrestrained: But happy and blessed is he who keeps the law (of God)*" (Proverbs 29:18 AMPC). This was overwhelmingly the most popular response in the survey, and so let's briefly take a look at understanding the true source of our happiness.

> Happiness is a by-product of our faith obedience to God's Word.

How To Be Happy

Happiness is a by-product of our faith obedience to God's Word. Acting on God's Word from a heart of love for Him results in a place of happiness and contentment in our lives. I did not get saved (married to Jesus) to be happy. This is why so many so-called Christians are unhappy. Happiness comes in my walk with Jesus as I follow him in faith obedience.

Finding Wisdom And Gaining Understanding

Happy is the man who finds wisdom and a man who gains understanding (Proverbs 3:13 AMPC). Happiness does not come from finding "the right one" but is found in the wisdom and understanding that emanates from God. The source of happiness is our revelation of our heavenly Father and how we become more and more secure in that happiness as we walk in obedience to His Holy Word. Had Sue been looking to me as the source of her happiness on our honeymoon, she may have become depressed and suicidal! God was the source of her happiness, and I was the opportunity for hysterical laughter, which is still the case today. Happiness is the overflow of wisdom and understanding of my union with Christ. When I see by revelation who I am in Christ through simple faith, I get happy. How could knowing that we are married to Jesus make us anything but happy!

God's Correction

"Happy is the man God corrects..." (Job 5:17 NKJV). To a large extent, people refuse instruction from God's Word on how to be a husband and wife that pleases God and blesses each other. When we change our minds (repent) and receive God's correction in our thoughts and direction for our lives, we experience true happiness.

Kids And Happiness

"Children are a heritage from the Lord...happy is the man who has his quiver full of them..." (Psalm 127:3-5 NKJV). A quiver is

a case that traditionally holds five or seven arrows. So, this scripture is telling us that a man is happy when he has five or seven children! Wow, that is really different. Most people quiver at the mention of one! I'm not saying you have to have a whole passel of children; there are large quivers and small quivers. I am just pointing out that, contrary to popular opinion, children are a blessing. Through my union and active faith relationship with Jesus, I bear children like love, joy, peace, longsuffering, kindness, goodness, faithfulness, gentleness, and self-control (see Galatians 5:22-23). When these things are born out of my relationship with the Lord, I am happy.

ANSWER #2—"TO FIND MY VALUE AND WORTH." (WRONG ANSWER!)

We cannot find our worth in a spouse but *only* in Christ and the cross. Before Christ, we were held hostage by sin, Satan, and the powers of darkness. The ransom demand was the life of Jesus. Guess what?! God paid it and in full! We are not purchased with silver or gold but with the precious blood of Jesus (1 Peter 1:18-19). Let me say it again, God made Jesus, His only Son, a ransom for you and me. He gave His life for ours. We don't need to look anywhere else for our value or worth. The price God paid in sacrificing Jesus on the cross settles the question forever. My value and worth is found in my new identity in my marriage to Jesus, not Sue.

ANSWER #3—"TO COMPLETE ME." (WRONG ANSWER!)

I have thought this way in the past, and while our spousal relationship has a sense of fulfillment within it, no person can make us complete. Before marriage, we are no more "incomplete" than the apostle Paul was as a single man or Jesus was as Lord. *"For in Christ lives all the fullness of God in a human body. So you also are complete through your union with Christ, who is the head over every ruler and authority"* (Colossians 2:9-10 NLT). My marriage to Jesus brings completeness in me, not my marriage to Sue.

A good marriage is not two incomplete people coming together in order to become complete, any more than two unhappy people can get married and suddenly become happy. God's plan for marriage is two happy and complete people who know who they are in God, and when they are joined in marriage, they enjoy each other and God together. That's God's plan: Two imperfect—but whole—people coming together in a synergy within a newly formed unity where there is companionship and partnership in God's Kingdom. In that unity there is a newfound strength. One will put a thousand to flight; two, ten thousand (see Deuteronomy 32:30). We are simply stronger and better together than we are alone.

While Sue and I complement each other, only Jesus can complete us. In the unity of marriage, one plus one no longer equals two but ten. Sue and I are not twice as strong together, but rather ten times as strong in the grace of life. I can't begin to explain how much better we are with Jesus than without Him. Marriage to Him produces power that is destructive to the powers of darkness.

ANSWER #4—"TO GET OUT OF TROUBLE." *(WRONG ANSWER!)*

Holy cow! Marriage will only complicate or replicate your troubles. It cannot fix them. Marriage brings a whole new set of problems; it's just part of the territory as two different human

59

beings learn to live in unison. The institution of marriage itself does not solve problems. However, coming together and combining all our human resources and revelation knowledge of God's wisdom can enable us to effectively tackle and overcome our problems. *"But and if thou marry, thou hast not sinned; and if a virgin marry, she hath not sinned. Nevertheless such shall have trouble in the flesh: but I spare you"* (1 Corinthians 7:28).

There are also problems in the flesh. There are new challenges in our lives, in the natural, domestic realm. In this chapter, Paul celebrates the blessings and benefits of single life. If one can control his or her sexuality and not "burn with lust," single life has many advantages over marriage. Paul had a grace gift that empowered him to remain pure in his sexuality. I don't have that gift, so marriage is a good fit for me and so many others like me. While marriage helps with so many issues, it is not designed to be a "fix all" for our problems. Marriage opens the door to many blessings and benefits in our lives, but a "trouble free zone" is not one of them. The road to a successful, happy marriage is under constant construction. It is definitely work but well worth the labor!

> ***Two are better than one***, *because they have a good reward for **their labor***. *For if they fall, one will lift up his companion. But woe to him who is alone when he falls, for he has no one to help him up. Again, if two lie down together, they will keep warm; but how can one be warm alone? Though one may be overpowered by another, two can withstand him. And a threefold cord is not quickly broken* (Ecclesiastes 4:9-12 NKJV).

Many get saved to get out of trouble. While Jesus delivers us from all our destruction, Christianity is not a trouble-free zone either. With this marriage to Jesus comes persecution, trials, and afflictions. As we navigate the challenges of life, we now have Jesus, who is our wisdom (1 Corinthians 1:30) to guide us through the storms of life.

ANSWER #5—"I THOUGHT I'D GIVE IT TRY AND SEE HOW IT WENT." *(WRONG ANSWER!)*

Marriage is not a social experiment. It has a specific Creator, a specific definition, and a specific purpose for all mankind. God personally designed it, and God Himself is very protective of it as an institution. Marriage is more than a contract that we can exit. Taking vows together is a covenant, and a covenant is an unbreakable agreement. In the marriage covenant, two individual people become one. Marriage sanctifies our sexuality and expression

> While Jesus delivers us from all our destruction, Christianity is not a trouble-free zone either.

of sexual love. We don't "try it" and see how or where it goes. We enter a commitment unto death, and with God's help, we purpose in our hearts how it goes. Sue and I have determined that it will go well. We entered the covenant of marriage with shared commitment and understanding: "till death do us part." *"Marriage is honorable in all, and the bed undefiled: but whoremongers and adulterers God will judge"* (Hebrews 13:4).

Can you see God's sanctifying of marriage, our sexuality within marriage, and then the judgment of sexuality outside of marriage? While God is not punishing us for our sins or pouring wrath out on us, a day of judgment is coming. Sexual sins as well as all others will be judged at the appearing of Jesus and His Kingdom. This is what God has saved us from by creating marriage. There is only one definition of marriage, and because God created marriage, He gets to define it. Marriage is not whatever we decide we want it to be individually or collectively as a culture. It is not defined by anyone's personal opinion. It is not a matter of the "age of consent" and how much two people think they love each other. It doesn't matter what a president, or the supreme court, or you or I think; it only matters what God thinks and has declared in Holy Scripture.

Sexual Boundaries

In First Corinthians 5, a man was sleeping with his father's wife (his stepmother). I'm sure they were of the age of consent, and maybe they even thought it was love. Maybe they thought that their being together meant "love won." But Paul made it clear that it was wrong and sinful. When mothers have sex with sons, love does not win. Maternal love gets perverted and dies. When fathers sleep with daughters, love does not win, paternal love dies. Anything outside of God's definition of marriage brings death and destruction to the nuclear family, and our physical bodies as well. Paul encouraged us in First Corinthians 6:18 to, *"Flee fornication. Every sin that a man doeth is without the body; but he that committeth fornication sinneth against his own body."*

We are commanded to flee fornication (sex outside of our covenant of marriage). That's *flee*—not celebrate, flaunt, or encourage. When we commit fornication, we sin against our bodies inviting consequences of our sin to manifest in our bodies. All sin brings consequences. Every seed sown brings a harvest. Sexual sins have consequences affecting our bodies such as: sexual diseases, AIDS, broken relationships and emotional trauma. This doesn't even touch the surface of pains associated with sexual perversions.

We don't hear the truth about sex very much because the world wants to let it be a free- for-all. On the contrary, in order to really be free, we should run from sexual sin, not embrace, celebrate, or mandate that "free sex" is one of our human rights. Keeping our bodies for one person is a way of honoring marriage, ourselves, and our future spouse. It frees us to be open and intimate in a secure way. When we sleep with multiple partners, we dishonor marriage and diminish the beauty of sexual love. God created sex and us as sexual beings. Adam and Eve experienced the joy and pleasure of sexual love

> Sex did not contribute to the fall of man but rather suffered because of it.

within the safe boundaries of marriage. Sex did not contribute to the fall of man but rather suffered because of it. There is no "safe sex" outside of marriage as God ordained it to be.

Understanding Sex

Sexuality can only be well-handled within proper boundaries. Outside the covenant of marriage it becomes a destructive, harmful force that damages relationships. Adultery, fornication, and incest (as well as other sexual misconduct) have a whole host of emotional, relational, and physical repercussions. Outside of marriage, sex becomes trivial and shallow. Casual sex actually demeans a person, because there is no devotion involved with it.

Sex is amoral and is only good or bad depending on how we relate to it. It also has a huge effect on our heart. Water is amoral and is good or bad depending on how we relate to it. We can't live three or four days without water or three or four minutes under it. Within the confines of the river banks, water is life to a city. Outside the banks, during a flood, it can destroy a city and many lives. Fire is amoral and is a blessing in the fireplace. Within its designated boundaries, it is a blessing and brings warmth to all in the room. Outside of the fireplace, it becomes a destructive force that can destroy possessions and every life it touches. (I should know, and I'm about to tell you why.)

Fireplace—Blessing or Not?

Several years ago, I almost destroyed our home with fire. Sue loves a fireplace, and one night a romantic streak hit me—I figured I would do something to bless her. So, I decided to put a small wood stove in our bedroom. This was serious business, because it meant building a rock wall and cutting a hole in the roof. I was definitely looking for a reward. I worked hard all day (with some help) and managed to get this beautiful white stove with gold trim all set in place. The love flame was burning, and it was time to put my plan of romance into action.

When I bought the fireplace, I also purchased some three-pound presoaked logs. I'm from Florida, so I had no idea what a presoaked log was or how they worked. I put one presoaked log in and started it, but I decided it wasn't enough of a flame, so I put a second log in. Sue gently warned me not to, but did I listen? Of course not! I thought, *Surely, she doesn't know what she is talking about and I want a FIRE!* Well, we definitely had a fire. As the flames grew larger, smoke started filling the room. I proceeded to use the fancy tools that came with the fireplace and started beating on the logs, hoping to break them down, separate the wood, and calm the fire that was now climbing the wall. Those of you that are familiar with presoaked logs can well imagine what was beginning to happen. You guessed it; the gasses were igniting and the flame was growing—not spreading out and dying, as I had hoped.

Something had to be done, so I grabbed a spray bottle from our bathroom—it had water in it—and I started squirting. It looked like I was charging hell with a water pistol; it was not a lot of help. What was Sue doing during this whole time you ask? She was laughing. She went to the kitchen to get a pitcher full of water and proceeded to put out the fire. Can I just say that romance went right out the door! Thank heaven nothing was damaged (except my ego, of course). My well-laid out plan to be a blessing—and to appear as a masterful lover, I must admit—almost turned into a disaster. The point is, our "coming together" was to be felt as a treasure, a holy, revered event. Sex is a blessing, and it is good with commitment, but it becomes meaningless when we treat it casually. God knew what He was doing when he designed sex to be embraced by a holy pledge. Sex in marriage is a beautiful thing.

The nuclear family and sexual love expressed within the safety of marriage is what God ordained from the beginning. He did so for good reason—it's healthy for our bodies, souls, and other relationships. Adultery and other forms of sexual perversions are damaging and harmful to others. You may not like to hear it, but sex outside of marriage hurts people and perverts things that are near and dear to the heart of God. As we look at the creation and purpose of marriage, let's not forget all of this is *"a great mystery: but I speak concerning the relation of Christ and the church"* (Ephesians 5:32). The devil would love to pervert and destroy the symbol of marriage because he hates the spiritual relationship we have with Jesus as our Husband. You can be sure that Jesus is faithful to you as His bride (the Church) above all else. As His wife, we need to learn to be faithful to Him above all else.

Over the years, I've contemplated the results of my marriage survey, and it caused me to look at my own marriage to Sue. I wanted to make sure she and I understood the purpose of marriage and either adjust, improve, or grow in wisdom in our understanding of Jesus and His love for His bride. When the purpose of marriage is understood, the purpose of God saving us is not only understood, but our relationship with Jesus grows in meaning and fulfilment. Jesus did not save us or become one spirit with our spirits just so we could be happy. Through our relationship and fellowship, there is a great joy as we live life together in companionship, but happiness is a by-product of our relationship with Him and faith obedience.

> The devil would love to pervert and destroy the symbol of marriage because he hates the spiritual relationship we have with Jesus as our Husband.

I didn't get saved to improve my self-esteem or feel value and worth in my flesh. My value and worth are in knowing how much Jesus loves me and gave Himself for me. While it is true that I'm complete in Jesus through the new birth, my wholeness is a means to an end to know how to love God and others. I didn't get saved or married to Jesus to get out of trouble but rather to have a Helper who will never leave or forsake me in any trouble I face in this life. I most certainly didn't get saved to "see how it works out" and determine if I stay or go. I'm committed until death... bringing us together in a new way and dimension. I realized that this is exactly how Jesus feels about being married to us.

CHAPTER 6

THE PURPOSES
OF MARRIAGE

*And the LORD God said, "It is not good that man should be alone; I will make him a **helper comparable to him**."*
—Genesis 2:18 NKJV

We know now that marriage was created and constructed by God. We see that a husband is a type of Christ, and everything said about a husband points to Christ. We also see that a wife is a type of the Church, and her role and assignments ordained by God teach us as the Church how to respond to Jesus. Let's start from the beginning and break down the purpose of marriage and unveil this divine union.

1. COMPANIONSHIP/PARTNERSHIP

The first purpose of marriage is companionship. God knew that Adam needed a partner, a "helpmeet," in the grace of life. Notice the process of finding this awesome helper that would be compatible and comparable to him.

> *Out of the ground the Lord God formed every beast of the field and every bird of the air, and brought them to Adam to see what he would call them. And whatever Adam called each living creature, that was its name. So Adam gave names to all cattle, to the birds of the air, and to every beast of the field. But for Adam there was not found a **helper comparable to him*** (Genesis 2:19-20 NKJV).

Verse 19 is simply a restating of the creation account in Genesis 1. On day six, God created the animals first (Genesis 1:24-25) and man last (Genesis 1:26-28). Man was the apex of all creation, created in God's image and likeness. He was God's "crown jewel," and given authority and dominion with glory and honor over all of God's beautiful creation (Psalm 8:5-6). Genesis 2 opens with the seventh day, a day of rest. Man's work in the garden was to come out of that Sabbath rest. Work, taking dominion over creation, and naming animals did not begin until the eighth day. Genesis 2:19 is not contradicting the creation order of chapter one (the animals being created first and then Adam), it is simply restating how God formed the animals out of the ground as well as man (Genesis 2:7). Chapter one gives the order of creation, and chapter two holds the details. None of chapter two occurred until after the seventh day of rest (Genesis 2:1-3).

Now that we know God created Adam (and all mankind) in His image, we can be sure that we are absolutely a reflection of Him. How awesome is that?! Another way for me to say it is that man—both male and female together—make up the image of God. In one way, God is neither male or female, and in another sense, He is both male and female in perfect harmony. Please don't misunderstand, I'm not saying that God is male and female in the way that we physically are. John 4:24 makes it very clear that *"God is Spirit."* I'm simply saying that God simultaneously embodies all the character traits that are masculine and feminine.

God, in His wisdom and benevolence, approached Adam with the revelation of his need for someone to walk alongside him. He identified a problem and then, as He always does, provided the solution. First, almost like a living picture book, He presented visuals by bringing all of the animals in pairs—male and female—to Adam. God created male and female to continue the species. He brought them to Adam to reveal to him his need for a helpmeet. After naming the animals for who knows how long, he realized each animal had a helpmeet, one of their own kind that was like them but different, except him. While Adam knew from creation that he was different, he now realized that he was alone. Since no helpmeet was found outside of Adam, God ventured inside of him to bring forth a blessed counterpart—one of his own kind but different. Now comes the first operation in the world, and God as the Master Physician opens Adam's side and brings forth this helper that would be compatible to him.

> I'm simply saying that God simultaneously embodies all the character traits that are masculine and feminine.

She Was Inside!

> *And the Lord God caused a **deep sleep** to fall on Adam, and he slept; and He took one of his ribs, and closed up the flesh in its place. Then the rib which the Lord God had taken from man He made into a woman, and He brought her to the man. And Adam said: "This is now bone of my bones and flesh of my flesh; she shall be called Woman, **because she was taken out of Man**"* (Genesis 2:21-23 NKJV).

Notice the verse says, "she was taken out of Man." She (female) was on the inside of Adam. You cannot be taken out of where you have not been. Female was on the inside of the first man, Adam.

> " **Female was on the inside of the first man, Adam.** "

Whatever female is, was present on the inside of Adam before this operation. We know there is more to a woman than her body (So we've been told numerous times! Keep yourself full of humor here!) and whatever that is (female) was on the inside of him. Don't read that lightly. Really, let that sink in for a moment.

We have nothing in the natural to draw off of to help us understand and truly comprehend the truth that : "she was in him." Male and female were created on the same day (the sixth day), on the *inside* of Adam. God then puts him into a deep sleep. "Woman" was created days later and brought back by God to Adam. This is different than anything I was ever taught and a profound part of original creation. It has deep meaning to marriage, and we will see later, the great mystery, Christ and the Church (new creation).

This idea of female inside of the first man Adam is repeated in Genesis 5:1-2.

> *This is the book of the generations of Adam. In the day that God created man, in the likeness of God made he him; Male and female created he them; and blessed them, and called **their name Adam**, in the **day when they were created.***

Notice "male and female" were created on the same day; not man (Adam) and woman (Eve). As male and female, God called their (plural) name Adam (singular). He did this on the sixth day (singular) when they (plural, male and female) were created. *"...In the likeness of God made He him, male and female created he them."* Why is it stated this way? Because on the inside of him (Adam) was them—male and female. Again, woman was created days later and was brought back to Adam, the man, and they become one flesh again in the marriage covenant. Adding great weight to this principle, Paul reaffirms this truth in Second Corinthians 11:8-9 where he states: *"For the first man didn't come from woman, but the first woman came from man. And man was not made for woman, but woman was made for man"* (NLT). That sure has been messed up and misapplied by many. There are things said such as "Yea, the first woman came from the first man so submit woman—clean that deer, change that oil in my car, and get me a glass of tea before Jesus returns." We need to be very careful in how we treat women and our wives and daughters. While the first woman came from the first man, every man since that time has come from woman, and there have been billions of them (thanks Mom!). Now, back to my point.

In the creation of Eve (woman), we are told that God took a "rib" from Adam and from the rib, and rib alone, He "made" the woman. He made woman and brought her to Adam. God broke the bone and marrow down and fashioned Eve. The marrow in the bone is what produces the blood, so Adam's very DNA was in her. She was quite literally bone of his bone. When he looked at her, she looked back. He saw himself in her. She was of him and from him, so he called her *wo-man*. It's no accident God made him name all the animals before this operation, because once woman (Eve) was presented, the "naming animal game" was over. It was time to leave and cleave. (That will hit you later!)

> Women are different because God spent special time building her.

Woman was Built

The word "made" in the Hebrew is the same word translated "built" (Strong's—H-1129 BANAH). Women are different because God spent special time building her. She is much more complex in her perspective (sorry guys, that happens to be a good thing), and she may require much more attention in areas of basic needs. Men and women are different, and women are to be treated with honor, respect, and care. To treat or speak the same way to a woman as you would a man, in some settings, would be disrespectful. There are hundreds of differences, and it is sad how women are mistreated in our culture because of a minority of voices claiming men and women are the same. We are not. Different doesn't mean lesser than or inferior to; it means different. Different is a physical thing, but it is also emotional and psychological. Obviously, we look different, (you have to have help to miss this one), but we also think and feel differently. At the same time, we need to understand that all of us are equally loved and valued by God.

Love as a Bond

We bond differently too. Men bond by respect and women bond by emotional, romantic love; thus, the commandment from God to love and respect.

> *Nevertheless let each one of you in particular so **love** his own wife as himself, and let the wife see that she **respects** her husband* (Ephesians 5:33 NKJV).

If 100,000 romance books are sold every year and 99,990 are sold to women, the 10 probably bought by men are gifts for their wives. Since God made us, He knows how each spouse works and what their basic needs are. Husbands are commanded to love their wives as themselves because that's what bonds us—men being men and taking care of things.

Respect as a Bond

A wife is to respect her husband; that's what will cause him to bond to her. So, love and respect are always at work in a marriage, and we do well when we flow with that because that helps us connect like we were designed to do. Men need respect, and women need love. We are to be as one in marriage as male and female were in Adam in original creation with love and respect in our union.

Different Is Good

God planned for us to enjoy our differences, not resent them and allow them to divide us. Unfortunately, our culture wants to blur the distinctions between men and women. It desires to make gender and sexuality a blank slate on which we can say; "Identity as this or desire to be that depending on what day of the week it is." Frankly, that is not of God, nor is it right. A person can rebel and act like he or she is "a free spirit," but there is no way the person can be free apart from his or her divine design and God's will within the gender assignment.

> God planned for us to enjoy our differences, not resent them and allow them to divide us.

God made boys and girls—nothing else! He assigned you to be you—a boy or a girl, a person with a special program, literally formed and traceable in your genetic DNA code. The Scriptures declare that "life is in the blood" (Genesis 9:4), and blood never lies. If there is a "Y" chromosome, "it's a boy"; if no "Y" chromosome, "it's a girl." No great mystery there—just biological fact. Because male and female were one on the inside of Adam, there can be traits of male in female or female in male, but this shouldn't create gender confusion. Overlapping traits of male and female simply testify of how unified male and female were in original creation.

Gender Confusion

Just because a man has some feminine traits, doesn't mean he is a female; nor do some masculine traits in a female make her a male. We should never judge or criticize someone for having feminine or masculine traits opposite their created gender, nor should we accuse God falsely of His gender assignment of male and female. He brought "female" out of man because He showed Himself as both male and female, both with wonderful attributes.

Rib and Woman

In Genesis 2:22 (NLT) we read; *"Then the Lord God made a woman from the rib...."*

The word "rib" in the original language of Hebrew means "other side" (Strong's—H-6763 TSELA). Woman is the other side of man. I'm not implying or suggesting that female in the marriage relation is to be hidden from public view or hidden behind the man, quite the contrary. Woman, in my estimation and in most cases, is the better side of man. Woman is the "other side" of man that causes him to be sensitive. Sometimes a woman's need for conversation is joked about. Now, I am all for humor in life, but at the root of things, woman's communication is part of her ability to understand her husband's thoughts and feelings and support him, precisely because she came (in creation) from within him. She is an asset, and she is an important and influential helpmeet. She belongs beside—not over or under her husband. She came from a rib (side), not a part of his skull or toe. She was the very last thing God created in all of creation, and I believe God saved the best for last. She was, and still is to this day, very special within all of creation. (I hope Sue reads this!)

> Overlapping traits of male and female simply testify of how unified male and female were in original creation.

Man and Woman Connection

Think about the names for woman in connection to man. In the Hebrew language, man is IYSH and woman is *ISH*-HAH. In the English it is wo-*man*; s-*he*; fe-*male*; *he*-r. I'm not saying women are to be dependent on men; I'm saying we are connected.

> *...She shall be called Woman because **she was taken out of Man*** (Genesis 2:23 NKJV).

While we do not "complete" each other, we certainly, and profoundly, enhance and complement each other. Man and woman are intended to bring out the best in each other. We read in Ecclesiastes that, *"Two are better than one, because they have a good reward for their labor. For if they fall, one will lift up his companion. But woe to him who is alone when he falls...."* (Ecclesiastes 4:9-10 NKJV). The first purpose of marriage is companionship and partnership. Woman has an identity with man. The Church came from Jesus and has a new identity with Him, and as Christians we work alongside Jesus as co-laborers. We are not over or under Him but from His very side. We are called *Christ-ians* because we came from Christ.

> Man and woman are intended to bring out the best in each other.

2. ONE FLESH PRINCIPLE

The second purpose of marriage is stated in this next verse and lets us know that becoming one flesh is an ongoing process.

*Therefore, a man shall leave his father and mother and be joined to his wife, and **they shall become one flesh**. And were both naked, the man and his wife, and were not ashamed* (Genesis 2:24-25 NKJV).

In marriage there is a harmonious synergy of male and female, where we are better together than we are apart. But how do we know the Genesis account applies to us and not just to Adam and Eve? Because of verse 24: *"Therefore, shall a man leave his father and mother and shall cleave to his wife."*

Adam and Eve had no father or mother. They were direct creations of God. Adam came from the *"dust of the earth,"* and Eve came from *"the rib"* of Adam. Neither came from an earthly father or mother. They were created in full maturity, not babies. God skipped the childhood and teenage stages (sounds unfair to me as a father of four children). This passage is speaking of you and me who do leave father and mother when we marry and become "one flesh" with our spouses. This is why the original blueprint for marriage applies to us thousands of years later.

Secondly, Jesus, thousands of years later in Mark 10, refers back to this, speaking into Israel's marriages. In this we also can see that Jesus connected their marriages to Adam and Eve and now ours (see Mark 10:6-9).

The bond of husband and wife is greater than that of father and mother and even of child. Think about that. We had a genetic connection to our father, and a life-sustaining connection to our mother for nine months in the womb. Each and every one of us early in life were one with our mother. At birth, the life-giving umbilical cord was cut, but still we remained close and bonded to her. There is a real link between mother and child—until marriage. The "one-flesh" principle (bonding of husband and wife) is even greater than the bond of parent and child.

At marriage, the parental cord is cut, and the bride and groom become one. Within this union, there is to be safety and security as in a covenant relationship, which is an unbreakable promise. That is why the traditional vows use the phrase, "till death do us part" and why divorce is so painful to God. God hates divorce because He loves us so much, and He knows what a separation like that does to people. Because of God's amazing grace, there is life after divorce, but He doesn't want any of us to experience that kind of pain after becoming one flesh. There really is a mystical union of male and female that affects us in a deep and profound way in our hearts. It's like two pieces of paper glued together; they become one and it is impossible to cleanly separate the two again. It is simply impossible to pull them apart without some damage to both pieces. Only death is to separate husband and wife, but marriage is to separate child and parent. Marriage is a covenant, not just a contract, between male and female. Malachi makes this very clear and plain. *"Yet you say, 'For what reason?' Because the Lord has been witness between you and the wife of your youth, with whom you have dealt treacherously; Yet she is your companion and your wife by covenant"* (Malachi 2:14 NKJV).

"Your wife by covenant" speaks of an unbreakable union. A covenant is an unbreakable vow and can only be broken by death. Marriage in this passage is referred by God as a covenant. The purpose of marriage is expressed in "she is your companion" (first purpose of marriage) and "wife of your covenant" (second purpose). The one-flesh principle is the coming together of two

separate lives glued together like two separate pieces of paper now becoming one.

This one-flesh principle includes sex but involves more than just sexual love. We have a synergy together in life that makes us stronger together than alone. Marriage is a covenant bond where we are no longer two, but now "one flesh." A husband and wife are as one in marriage as male and female were one in Adam. In original creation male and female were in one accord in Adam. In marriage, husband and wife live in one accord and are heirs together of the grace of life. Our union with Christ is as profound

> We came from Jesus and are united to Him in holy matrimony.

and more so in becoming one spirit with the Lord. There is a synergy when grace and faith come together.

As a believer, I am growing in my understanding and experiencing my union with Christ. We will never be separated from Jesus. We came from Jesus and are united to Him in holy matrimony. As we go through life's challenges, we must embrace the grace that is only found in Jesus. Many times we feel alone in times of trouble, but Jesus is with us to comfort, empower, and deliver us as our Husband.

3. SEXUAL PURITY

The third purpose of marriage is to experience and enjoy sexual love. God created us sexual beings, and sex was enjoyed by Adam and Eve before sin entered the world. Notice Paul's clear instructions to the believers at Corinth and their call to sexual purity:

"... It is good for a man not to touch a woman. Nevertheless, to avoid fornication, let every man have his own wife, and let every woman have her own husband" (1 Corinthians 7:1-2).

We don't have to be ferreting about in bars or parties to find someone to be with. We don't have to be creating all the emotion and physical damage having sex without commitment. The brokenness created emotionally and the risk of serious sexual diseases is unnecessary. Marriage is where sexual love is intended to be experienced and enjoyed. Sex is a good thing—it is a gift from God.

It is, however, a gift with boundaries. It is to be savored within the covenant protection of a safe and comforting intimacy within marriage. We should be celebrating this aspect of marriage, not flaunting sexual perversion and fornication. Consider the following instructions from Jesus, our Husband, *"...Honor marriage, and guard the sacredness of sexual intimacy between wife and husband..."* (Hebrews 13:4 MSG). *"Run from sexual sin!..."* (1 Corinthians 6:18 NLT).

One of the purposes of marriage is to avoid sexual perversion.

> *Now regarding the questions you asked in your letter. Yes, it is good to abstain from sexual relations. But because there is so much **sexual immorality**, each man should have his own wife, and each woman should have her own husband. The husband should fulfill his wife's sexual needs, and the wife should fulfill her husband's needs* (1 Corinthians 7:1-3 NLT).

That all speaks of the joy of sexual love within marriage. Monogamous intimacy is the plan of God within marriage. Jesus desires the same monogamous spiritual intimacy with us, His bride. He doesn't want us having spiritual affairs or committing spiritual adultery with other lovers (gods). There is a spiritual commitment in our relationship with Jesus that requires the worship of Him and Him alone. He has a jealous love for us that we will look at in greater depth in another chapter.

4. A GODLY SEED

The fourth purpose of marriage is to have children. God likes children and has partnered with us as husband and wife to bring forth children. *"Then God blessed them, and God said to them, 'Be fruitful and multiply; fill the earth and subdue it...'"* (Genesis 1:28 NKJV).

Adam and Eve were charged with having children to fill the earth. In the book of Malachi, God said that He had some issues with His people and was not very pleased with them. He then explains the reason or purpose of marriage:

> There is a spiritual commitment in our relationship with Jesus that requires the worship of Him and Him alone.

*Yet you say, "For what reason?" Because the Lord has been witness between you and the wife of your youth, with whom you have dealt treacherously; Yet she is your **companion** and your wife by **covenant**. But did He not make them one, having a remnant of the Spirit? **And why one? He seeks godly offspring.** Therefore, take heed to your spirit, and let none deal treacherously with the wife of his youth* (Malachi 2:14-15 NKJV).

God made us to bear a "godly offspring." Many say they don't want to bring kids into such a dark world, but they don't know that it's been darker and a lot worse in previous generations. History doesn't begin with our generation; there has been a colossal story complete with battle scenes going on since the Garden of Eden. The world has been dark from the days of the flood, when the earth was filled with evil. Only eight people were righteous on the whole planet. In the days of Sodom and Gomorrah, only Lot and his family were righteous. Terrorism, tyranny, and slavery have been the norm for centuries as well as deep poverty and all manner of oppression.

Our children are to be a part of the solution rather than the problem, so we are highly accountable for their training. There is a special love God has for children, and I believe it's because they are the only thing He hasn't created independent of man—Adam and Eve were fully grown, mature adults at creation. He intended for them to rule and fill the earth; He intended that Adam's descendants would know how to rule and carry on the process. Having and raising children in the nurture and admonition of the Lord is a part of the purpose of marriage.

Through our union with Christ and now our faith response to Jesus, we are bearing fruit and filling the earth with God's glory. Ministry is literally being birthed out of our relationship with the Lord. All our works (fruit) are coming out of our love for Jesus and now others. We were saved to bring forth new fruit of the Kingdom and our fruit remain (see John 15:16). What is coming out of our lives through Christ is making a difference.

5. THE GREAT MYSTERY OF OUR UNION WITH CHRIST

The fifth purpose of marriage is to reflect Christ and the Church (Ephesians 5:32).

Everything I've said connects to Christ and His Church. While there is a domestic side to marriage, it is the spiritual side that God wants to reveal. Our new identity as the bride of Christ ensures that the full recovery of everything lost in the fall is now recovered in the faith. Imagine the marvelous possibilities of being married to Jesus!

> Our new identity as the bride of Christ ensures that the full recovery of everything lost in the fall is now recovered in the faith.

In the next chapter, we will compare the marriage of Adam and Eve in original creation to Jesus and the Church in the new creation.

CHAPTER 7

CHRIST AND THE CHURCH

*This is a **great mystery**, but it is an illustration
of the way **Christ and the church are one**.*
—EPHESIANS 5:32 NLT

Paul, in explaining this beautiful union between Christ and His Church, calls it a great mystery. Within that marriage there is much power and fulfillment. God wants to bring out the essentials of covenant marriage because this helps us understand what pure Christianity is all about—a new covenant with Jesus.

Jesus has entered into a covenant with me even as I entered into a covenant with Sue. Just as Sue and I are an example of husband

> God wants to bring out the essentials of covenant marriage because this helps us understand what pure Christianity is all about—a new covenant with Jesus.

and wife working together, we are also an example of Jesus as Husband working together with His wife, the Church. And just as I yearn to be with Sue, Jesus yearns to be with us.

God has always loved us, even when it surely seemed that we couldn't care less about Him. Israel is a good example of this. He married the Nation of Israel at Sinai (the mountain where the Ten Commandments were given), and He was adamant about being the source for all of their needs—spiritual, emotional, and physical. He told them over and over again that He would be there in every situation, and He would supply anything they had need of—food, clothing, shelter, peace, confidence, security. When they were in the wilderness, He gave them manna from heaven to sustain them. There was a rock that Moses struck with his rod and water came out to quench their thirst and take care of their livestock. A cloud came over them in the day to shield them from the heat of the desert, and a fire went before them by night to protect them from the cold. He protected them from Pharaoh by drowning his army in the Red Sea. God was a steadfast Husband in every way, but Israel was a wayward wife.

The story of Hosea and Gomer illustrates how Israel refused to remain monogamous, and how they kept getting distracted and drawn toward other affections. God used Gomer as an example of Israel's behavior and Hosea an example of His own perseverance. The book of Hosea actually confused me for years until I understood that God was *married* to Israel. Hosea was a type of God as a husband, and Gomer was a type of Israel, as a wife.

When the Lord first began speaking to Israel through Hosea, he said to him, "Go and marry a prostitute, so

that some of her children will be conceived in prostitu-
tion. This will illustrate how **Israel has acted like a**
prostitute *by turning against the Lord and worship-*
ing other gods... (Hosea 1:2 NLT).

How weird does that sound? Marry a prostitute? Doesn't
sound like good counsel to give a godly man in choosing a wife.
Hosea and Gomer had children, but still she could not be faithful to him. She slept with many lovers, and she had children out
of prostitution. She was so messed up and skewed in her thinking
that she kept acting disloyal and unfaithful to Hosea her husband. Then God says to the man of God, *"...bring charges against*
Israel—your mother—for she is no longer my wife, and I am no
longer her husband... (Hosea 2:2 NLT). Then in verse 8 He says,
"She doesn't realize it was I who gave her everything she has—the
grain, the new wine, the olive oil; I even gave her silver and gold. But
she gave all my gifts to Baal" (Hosea 2:8 NLT).

God kept giving Israel everything, but at one point, He had to
stop. Israel was ungrateful and wandering, and she was not getting
the message. So He put her away and was no longer an active husband to her.

In Jeremiah 3 we find some of the most alarming words in
Scripture. Jeremiah picks up on the theme of Hosea and continues to use the picture of marriage and unfaithfulness in marriage
when speaking of Israel's spiritual adultery.

"If a man divorces a woman and she goes and mar-
ries someone else, he will not take her back again, for
that would surely corrupt the land. But you have **pros-**
tituted yourself with many lovers, *so why are you*

*trying to come back to me?" says the Lord. "Look at the shrines on every hilltop. Is there any place you have not been defiled by your **adultery with other gods?** ... **Like a wife who commits adultery,** Israel has worshiped other gods on every hill and under every green tree. I thought, 'After she has done all this, she will return to me.' But she did not return, and her faithless sister Judah saw this. **She saw that I divorced faithless Israel because of her adultery.** But that treacherous sister Judah had no fear, and now she, too, has left me and **given herself to prostitution"*** (Jeremiah 3:1-8 NLT).

Jesus said adultery was the only justification for divorce (Matthew 5:32). This seems unbelievable, but God actually gave Israel a bill of divorce! Wow, that's heavy. He was a Husband to her and called her an "adulteress wife." Can you imagine the reaction in most circles if you said, "God has been divorced?" Someone might respond by saying, "How could God be married to a Jew today then, because divorce and remarriage is not allowed? Death is the only thing that releases us from a marriage, and that is when we are able to marry another and not be called an adulterer" (see Romans 7:1-6). You see that death in Jesus and the death we all experience at the cross (see Galatians 2:20/Romans 6:6) Isaiah, as a third witness of Israel's unfaithfulness speaks of her being put away. *"Thus says the LORD: 'Where is the certificate*

> This seems unbelievable, but God actually gave Israel a bill of divorce!

of your mother's divorce, Whom I have put away? Or which of My creditors is it to whom I have sold you? For your iniquities you have sold yourselves, And for your transgressions your mother has been put away" (Isaiah 50:1 NKJV).

Back to Jeremiah and his call for Israel to repent of sins and spiritual adultery so God would be merciful and take her back. "*Israel...thought nothing of committing adultery by worshipping idols made of wood and stone.... O Israel my faithless people, come home to me for I am merciful. I will not be angry with you forever. Only acknowledge your guilt. Admit that you rebelled against the Lord your God and committed adultery against him by worshipping idols under every green tree. Confess that you refused to listen to my voice...*" (Jeremiah 3:9-13 NLT).

God brought Israel back, because He could never stop yearning for her. In the end of Hosea's allegory, Gomer had sunk to her lowest point; she was being sold at an auction for next to nothing. She'd brought this desecration upon herself, (just like we often do), but Hosea was there to buy her, to give her another chance at a good life. Hosea 3:1 says, "*Then the Lord said to me, 'Go and love your wife again, even though she commits adultery with another lover. This will illustrate that the Lord still loves Israel, even though the people have turned to other gods and love to worship them*'" (NLT).

The Jews in Jesus' day were completely disloyal to God, yet Jesus paid for them to have a new life. He paid for their sins and unbeknown to the Jews at the time, for ours too. At the get-go, God proclaimed allegiance to the Jews, and then expanded that allegiance to the whole world—to whomever would come to Him in betrothal. Regardless of our infidelities, He loves us all tenderly and always through Jesus, who remains our Husband, the One we lean on.

THE NEW COVENANT (MARRIAGE)

Up until the crucifixion of Jesus at the cross, mankind was married to their old sinful nature. The Old Testament law highlighted mankind's sinful nature but did not change it. The marriage of the Jews and God under this law was not a happy marriage. Both the Jews and the Gentiles, through their crucifixion with Christ at the cross, died to the old man and entered a new covenant. The death of the old man released us to be married to another, to Jesus. The first contract (the law with only the Jews under the old covenant) was canceled out by the second contract (the new covenant). Grace! The new covenant was addressed to the people of Israel and Judah. Jesus was sent to the Jew first and then to the Gentiles (people of the world). God has brought both Jew and Gentile together as one in Jesus.

> The marriage of the Jews and God under this law was not a happy marriage.

> But when God found fault with the people, he said: "The day is coming, says the Lord, when I will make a new covenant with the **people of Israel** and Judah. This covenant will not be like the one I made with their ancestors when I took them by the hand and led them out of the land of Egypt. They did not remain faithful to my covenant, so I turned my back on them

*says the Lord. But this is the new covenant I will make with the **people of Israel** on that day, says the Lord: I will put my laws in their minds, and I will write them on their hearts. I will be their God, and they will be my people. And they will not need to teach their neighbors, nor will they need to teach their relatives, saying, 'You should know the Lord.' For everyone, from the least to the greatest, **will know me** already. And I will forgive their wickedness, and I will never again remember their sins." When God speaks of a "new" covenant, it means he has made the first one obsolete. It is now out of date and will soon disappear* (Hebrews 8:8-13 NLT).

In the New Covenant, Jesus mentions the people of Israel and that "all will know me." This kind of *know* is a term used in Scripture that refers to the intimate physical relationship between a husband and wife. It speaks of a relationship that results in the bearing of children. It is out of our personal faith relationship with Jesus that we bear much fruit (John 15:1-3). Jesus has saved us and joined Himself to us and desires now our faithfulness to Him.

God has always wanted commitment and singleness of heart toward Him. With a godly jealousy, He has always been jealous over us. He wants us to look to Him and Him alone for every single need we have. Our devotion to Him is to be as one of a godly wife to her husband. Until I understood the faithfulness within marriage of a husband and wife, I didn't understand how Jesus longs for my loyalty in true and pure worship of Him. He wants me to look to Him and trust Him as the One who meets all my needs in this life. Marriage is symbolic of something holy. It is a mystery hidden in God—a great treasure that unveils our union with Christ and what that union affords us.

ADAM VS. JESUS

There exists a correlation between Adam and Jesus as well as Eve and the Church. Let's investigate these parallels.

Adam:

> *And the Lord God said, it is not good that the man should be **alone**; I will make him an **help meet for him*** (Genesis 2:18).

Adam, the first man, was alone but not lonely. God promised a helper that would be compatible for Him.

Jesus:

Paul refers to Jesus as the second man and the last Adam in First Corinthians 15:45, 47. Jesus, like Adam, was alone but not lonely. God has a plan for Jesus as well and would create a helper that was compatible to the Lord (the Church).

Adam:

> *And out of the ground the Lord God formed every beast of the field, and every fowl of the air; and brought them unto Adam to see what he would call them; and whatsoever Adam called every living creature, that was the name thereof. And Adam gave names to all cattle, and to the fowl of the air, and to every beast of the field;*

*but for Adam there was **not found an help meet for him** (*Genesis 2:19-20).

Here we can see nothing within creation that was suitable for Adam as a helpmeet. One of his own kind but different.

Jesus:

Just like there was no helpmeet found among all the animals for Adam; there was no helpmeet for Jesus among all the different people groups. The Father brought all men to Jesus, there was not a helpmeet among them. He brought the Pharisees and Jesus called them snakes and vipers, tomb-stones full of dead men's bones. There was none among them of His kind. All of Israel was brought to the Lord, and He called them lost sheep without a shepherd. They were not of His kind. The Sadducees were brought, and they didn't believe in the resurrection; that's why they were so "Sad-you-see." (I couldn't help myself on that one.) How could they possibly be a "helpmeet"? The Gentiles were lost and without a covenant with God; no helpmeet was found among them either. So, what did the Father do? Let's look at what He did for Adam, and we will see what He did for Jesus.

> He wants us to look to Him and Him alone for every single need we have.

Adam:

*And the Lord God caused a **deep sleep** to fall upon Adam, and he slept: and he took one of his ribs, and closed up the flesh instead thereof; And the rib, which* *the Lord God had taken from man,* **made** *he a woman, and brought her unto the man. And Adam said, "This is now bone of my bones, and flesh of my flesh: she shall be called Woman,* **because she was taken out of Man"** *(Genesis 2:21-23).*

He found her in him and took her out for him.

Jesus:

Just as God had put the first Adam into a deep sleep, opened his side up, took a rib and built the woman. God also put the second man, the last Adam—Jesus— into a deep sleep at the cross (three days) and opened His side and took us out as "a rib" of Himself. We were in Christ at the cross just like Eve was in Adam in the garden. We were chosen "in Him" before the foundations of the world (see Ephesians 1:4). You and I (the bride) were in Him before the foundation of the world. Just as female was in Adam at the advent of the original creation, we were in Him at the cross and the birthing of the new creation.

> We were in Christ at the cross just like Eve was in Adam in the garden.

At the cross, a Roman soldier opened Jesus' side with a sword and blood and water came forth. Even as God took the rib of Adam and from it built Eve, God took us out of Jesus' side. We were found "in Him" and taken out "for Him" and brought to be united "to Him" to now rule and reign "with Him" (You may want to read that a couple of times. I did, and I wrote it). God brought Eve to Adam as a helpmeet, and in the same way, the Father has brought you and me to Christ as His "helpmeet" in the earth. In Matthew 16:18 Jesus said, *"...I will build my church; and the gates of hell will not prevail against it."* Verse 19 continues, *"And I will give unto thee the keys to the kingdom of heaven: and whatsoever thou shalt bind on earth shall be bound in heaven: and whatsoever thou shalt loose on earth shall be loosed in heaven."* In Eden God "built" woman, and now He is "building" the Church in the world. Adam and Eve had companionship and partnership; we now have companionship and partnership with Jesus on the earth. We are His helpmate (not His help mat). When Adam saw Eve, he saw himself in her and he said, "She shall be called *wo-man* because she was taken out of man." And contrary to all the animals, when he looked at her, she looked back. She was of his kind.

We, too, were taken out of Jesus. When Jesus looks at us, He sees Himself in us. We are *"born again, not of a corruptible seed but an incorruptible, through the word of God which lives and abides forever"* (1 Peter 1:23 NKJV). We are born again by the Spirit of God (John 3:6). A new creation (2 Corinthians 5:17). We are truly of and from Him. When Jesus looks at us, He wants us to look back; and now we are able to do that. Unlike Adam, who hid in shame, we can now look at Him with no sense of guilt or shame. We are of His kind in the new creation. We are able to leave the things of this world and cleave to Jesus as one spirit. We are called *Christians (Christ-ians)* because we came from Him. We were first called Christians at Antioch (Acts 11:25-26). This was a name given to

> When Jesus looks at us, He wants us to look back; and now we are able to do that.

the disciples (disciplined followers) by unbelievers. The believers were so united to Christ, having been conformed to His image, that all who saw them marveled and called them by a new name—*Christian.* We are completely united to Christ, though most of us have let the dynamic of this slip into a mere mental exercise and religious routine. We are spiritually so united with Jesus that we have Him in our new name. His spiritual DNA is in our spirit man. We have companionship, fellowship, and partnership with Him as heirs together of the grace of life (Romans 8:17). Notice how we came from God, and He prepared us as a bride for Christ even

> We are spiritually so united with Jesus that we have Him in our new name.

as He prepared Eve for Adam. *"And I John saw the holy city, new Jerusalem, coming down from God out of heaven, prepared as a bride adorned for her husband"* (Revelation 21:2). Or how we are born of God not of ourselves: *"But as many as received him, to them gave he power to become the sons of God, even to them that believe on his name: Which were born, not of blood, nor of the will of the flesh, nor of the will of man, but of God"* (John 1:12-13).

As believers we are born from above and of God. Spiritually, we come from heaven. In biblical terms, this makes the whole group of us a holy city. Matthew 5:14 speaks of a city set on a hill that cannot be hidden. This alludes to a light with altitude—lifted above the surrounding area, illuminating a wide expanse. It is a multitude of people intimately united with Jesus, elevated above the chaos and darkness that comes against us. We brandish a confidence that is not our own but a confidence in our Husband who has our back. So, we can be unafraid and shine with good works. In Scripture, the hill (or mountain) that we are set on is called "Zion." Zion was a place of grace, which is God's ability and favor. We shine on that mountain because we are dressed in the beauty of His grace. Israel entered into a covenant relationship with God at Sinai (a place of law). This was a covenant that had wrath and curses associated with any disobedience. Today, we have come to a completely different kind of mountain—one of grace and mercy. Christ has totally and completely delivered us from any curse of the law (see Galatians 3:13). While Jesus might not parade us through a Waffle House full of drunks and sleep-deprived truckers like I did Sue, I assure you that He is no less proud and excited about His bride than I was mine.

WE ARE LIKE HIM

*But ye are come unto mount Sion, and unto the city of the living God, the heavenly Jerusalem, and to an innumerable company of angels, to the general assembly and church of the firstborn, which are written in heaven, and to God the Judge of all, and to the **spirits of just men made perfect**, and to Jesus the mediator of the new covenant, and to the blood of sprinkling, that speaketh better things than that of Abel (Hebrews 12:22-24).*

Here we read of two different mountains with two different results. One was a covenant with death and condemnation; the other of life and righteousness (see 2 Corinthians 3:6-9). At Mount Sinai, three thousand people died in judgment and wrath for sins. On the day of Pentecost, three thousand people were justified and saved from their sins. As the Church, we have all come to Mount

Zion, the mountain of His tremendous grace and great love. It is God's grace—not law—that has saved us and now changes us and empowers us, day by day. The *"spirits of just men made perfect"* is a reference to our spirit that is righteous and truly holy because it is one spirit with Jesus in a marriage union. It's our spirit that is born-again and came from God, making us all new creations.

DOUBTING THOMAS

After the resurrection, Jesus appeared to His disciples and encouraged them; only Thomas was absent. Excitedly, they went and told Thomas that they had seen the Lord. Doubting, Thomas said he would not believe Jesus was alive or raised from the dead unless he put his finger in the nail prints in His hands and thrust his hand in His side. When Jesus appeared to him eight days later, he showed Thomas His nail prints and then let Thomas put his hand in His side (John 20:25-27). Jesus said, *"...Be not faithless, but believing"* (verse 27). Notice that, according to Scripture, His side was still open. Adam's side was sewn up after God removed the rib because God's work was complete. He had taken female out of Adam and brought Eve back to him. Jesus' side is still open because God is not finished "building His Church." I believe the bride (the Church) will be finished at the appearing of Jesus and His Kingdom, and His side will be sewn up because the end has come. Until then, there is room for our friends, families, and neighbors.

Adam:

> *Therefore shall a man **leave his father and his mother**, and shall cleave unto his wife: and they **shall be one flesh*** (Genesis 2:24).

Adam and Eve did not have a father and a mother. They both were a "hands on" creation of God and created in full maturity. Adam came from the dust of the earth and God breathed in him the breath of life. Eve came from Adam's rib and was "built" by God and brought to Adam as a mature, full-grown woman. Neither of them had a mom or a dad. It must have come as a shock to them for God to say "leave your mom and dad." What's a mom and a dad? Notice God said to leave our in-laws before any were on the planet! That's how bad they can be (Just kidding!). All joking aside, I probably had the sweetest mother-in-law on the planet. She suffered from dementia in the last several years of her life, forgetting everything including her children and their names. This was especially difficult on the entire family as you can well imagine. When she did communicate, she spoke of heaven and going there, so Sue's oldest brother spent as much time as possible reading the Scriptures to her. On one of our visits to Sue's hometown in Indiana, she, her brother, and I all went to visit Mom in the nursing home where she received care. Sure enough, she didn't know any of us. However, when she saw me, her face lit up, and she said "Jesus!" It was such a precious moment, and it touched our hearts in a deep and special way, Who wouldn't want to have a mother-in-law who thinks he's Jesus?!

What was God saying in the leaving of our father and mother? This is speaking of you and I and generations to come, because as I said, the parental cord of authority and direct oversight is broken at marriage. While Adam and Eve and the first marriage was unique in many ways, the creation and blessing of marriage was instituted for all mankind. Genesis 2:24 ties you and I into God's unique, unalterable plan for marriage. Jesus gave up His position in heaven, left the Father, and now is joined to us, His bride. He is now the Head of the Church, which is His body, flesh of His flesh and bone of His bones. Like Eve had the physical DNA of Adam, we have the spiritual DNA of Jesus. We are to leave and cleave to the Lord above all others. Jesus left His Father, and now we leave the world and look to our Husband for all things we need.

> "Jesus gave up His position in heaven, left the Father, and now is joined to us, His bride."

Adam:

> *And they were both **naked**, the man and his wife, and were not ashamed* (Genesis 2:25 NKJV).

There was no shame in their nakedness. They enjoyed their relationship with no hindrances or obstacles. I promise you, while Jesus sees our nakedness, He wants to remove all shame.

Jesus:

We are to be open and naked before the Lord and not ashamed, without condemnation or guilt, knowing that He will never condemn, ridicule, leave or forsake us. God has done such a beautiful and complete work at the cross in removing our sins and trespasses that we can have a relationship with Jesus free of our past, present, and even future failings. When I say naked, I really just mean transparent. Transparency requires full emotional and spiritual honesty—a nakedness with God, open with our thoughts, emotions, opinions, and actions, especially ones that are not so good. In this world and after our flesh, we simply fall short, and if He were to abandon us—look out! It would not be pretty. Fortunately, He will never go away, and He will always be calling for us. Our sole responsibility is to answer, even in our nakedness. We must never run from the Lord, but always to the Lord, especially when we fall or fail. We can come boldly to the throne of grace and obtain mercy in our time of need (see Hebrews 4:16). There is no greater time of need than in some type of nakedness. Remember He sees Himself in us.

AN EPIC LOVE

Adam's love for Eve was incredible, but Jesus' love for us is beyond description. Adam was not deceived in partaking of the forbidden fruit in the garden (1 Timothy 2:13-14). Eve ate of the tree and then offered some to Adam and he ate (Genesis 3:6). Why would he eat with his eyes wide open like that? I believe he knew Eve would die as God had declared and did not want to be without her. He loved her so much, he entered into her sin to be with her even if it meant death. Jesus loves us so much that He entered our humanity, became one of us (without sin). He willfully took our sins on the cross and died for us so we by faith could be with Him and He with us throughout eternity. What a great Husband. What a great mystery of His epic love for us. He knew exactly what going to the cross would cost, and He did it anyway. Because of this, He will be demonstrating His

> Adam's love for Eve was incredible, but Jesus' love for us is beyond description.

love and kindness toward us for the ages to come (see Ephesians

2:1-7). Nothing can or will separate Him from us. God the Father has joined us together and no person, thing, or event can put asunder what God has joined together (see Romans 8:32-39).

CHAPTER 8

JESUS OUR HUSBAND

*For I am **jealous** over you with **godly jealousy;***
for I have espoused you to one husband, that I
may present you a chaste virgin to Christ.
—2 Corinthians 11:2

Godly jealousy? How can there be anything godly in regard to jealousy? The love Jesus has for us is one that is jealous of us. Unlike jealousy of fallen man, God's jealousy for us is holy and pure. It is for our good and His Kingdom. Jealous is a part of God's nature revealed in His name. *"You must worship no other gods, for the Lord, whose very name is Jealous, is a God who is jealous about his relationship with you"* (Exodus 34:14 NLT).

> God wants the affection and full attention of our hearts.

That is absolutely amazing! God wants the affection and full attention of our hearts. He really loves me that much and desires a relationship free of the distraction of things and the cares of this life. His name reveals His nature and His character. His name is Jealous. He has a jealous love for us that He is unwilling to share with another. He wants to be the single source of everything in our lives. This is a positive, healthy, and wholesome commitment of His love for us. Many things in our world are competing for our love and affection (in some cases worship). A successful career can consume our lives and leave no room for the Lord. Sports and hobbies dominate our hearts and minds pushing Jesus to the sidelines. Social media and gadget addiction ensnare us, robbing us of the freedom Jesus brings into our lives. The latest sale and lust for things can leave little room for our Husband, Jesus.

Jesus wants us to have things, but He cautions us not to let "things" be the source of our joy and happiness. We can enjoy the blessings, but Jesus is our joy. He is the source of all good, even our capacity to enjoy what He gives. God wills for us to have a job, but our career is not the source of our prosperity. Jesus provides the way for that and the blessing in it, but a job is just a vehicle God uses as a means to provide for us and have extra to give to others (see Ephesians 4:28). God's prosperity in our lives supersedes our income from the job. When we recognize that Jesus is our source for prosperity, we'll never be limited by the income level of our job.

We truly have a marriage relationship where there is total devotion (worship), commitment, loyalty, and faithfulness to Jesus as Lord. Many of us claim to be Christians but our politics are our lord, money is lord, opinions of men are lord. What Jesus says in His Word is not final authority in our lives. I'm married to Jesus and not the politics of today. My marriage to Jesus is above anything and everything. Whatever you worship you will obey.

Whatever or whoever you love you will obey. Jesus said, *"If you love me, keep my commandments"* (John 14:15 NKJV). It is out of my love for Jesus that I have faith obedience to His Word. Other competing lovers may at times have our ear, but Jesus is to forever have our heart.

BACK IN THE DAY

Early in the ministry, things were tough. I remember doing meetings in small churches around our part of the country where the offering would be a box of canned goods or a couple of dozen eggs. What was more important was that we were grateful for it! At the same time, the Lord had put it on my heart to give my messages away for free, which in those days were cassette tapes (young people may have to google that one). So, the money we did have went to buying the supplies and equipment needed to fulfill that specific word from God. The bottom line was that we were so poor we could barely pay attention. Bleak didn't even begin to describe our financial condition in the natural.

> We truly have a marriage relationship where there is total devotion (worship), commitment, loyalty, and faithfulness to Jesus as Lord.

Money got so tight that discouragement seemed to be an ongoing battle. Praise God, we had enough to pay our rent and utilities, but there was literally nothing left for food or anything else. The one piece of gold (pun intended) we had was that we were being obedient in all that God had called us to do. Beyond that, we didn't know what to do, so we did the only thing that we knew; we prayed and determined to trust Him. Then there came a day of desperation, when we just knew something had to change or we would have to change our approach to ministry.

THE BREAKTHROUGH

Our oldest boy, Jeremy, was about three years old and, Jacob, his brother, was about one. It seems crazy to say, but we were actually eating our last meal. It is fun to laugh about it now—but it was not fun at the time. Sue was very discouraged. She saw that all we had were small portions of leftovers from previous meals. There was no stock in the pantry. There was no money coming in. The cupboards were bare, the refrigerator was empty, and a funny thing happened. Jeremy, in his innocence, completely ignorant of any of the difficulty that surrounded him, began to sing and proclaim gladness. As he helped Sue wash the dishes, he was singing, "This is the day.... This is the day...that the Lord has made...."

Sue immediately was encouraged to thank God for who He was and all He had done in our lives as our answer to discouragement. No matter how bad things looked, He had already provided for all of our needs according to His riches in glory. After all, that's what good husbands do! We were seeking the Kingdom first, and God's righteousness and all things would be added unto us and our family.

When I came home that evening we sat down to eat, each with a different meal in front of us on the table. I can't even begin to describe the guilt and condemnation that tried to grip my heart as I bowed my head to pray over our dinner. In the natural, this looked like the poor, broke Sheriff's version of the last supper. As I was praying, I had a battle in my mind concerning my responsibility to provide for my family, and I actually heard in my thoughts, First Timothy 5:8 that says, *"But if any provide not for his own, and specially for those of his own house, he hath denied the faith, and is worse than an infidel."*

I had come to a place in my life where it appeared that I was not able to meet the basic needs of my family. The ministry just wasn't generating the income to sustain us. My first thought was to go out and get a job outside of the ministry to help make ends meet. There's no shame in being bi-vocational in ministry. Many times, that can be essential for someone with a ministry call on their life. Even the great apostle Paul made tents on the side to keep from being chargeable to the burgeoning church at Corinth and at Thessalonica. I knew innately that there was nothing wrong with it, but I wrestled from the standpoint that I really believed I was doing what the Lord had told me to do.

With working upwards of 10-12 hours a day along with traveling and ministering in rural churches, I had no idea how I would find the time to do both. Then the Lord spoke to me as clear as I'm speaking to you right now. He said, "I am your Husband! You are my wife! For me to not provide for my own would mean that I have denied the faith and am worse than an infidel! I will not...I cannot deny the faith, and I will get provision to you if I have to bring it on the wings of ravens!"

Just like Satan did with Jesus in the wilderness, the enemy tried to use my knowledge of the Word of God to condemn me. God immediately stepped in and declared that He is personally accountable to every word in His Book. He has magnified His Word above His name. I was so certain at this point that God would provide for us somehow, some way. Well, Sue put the kids to bed, and we spent a couple of hours sharing what God had been showing us that day and praying together. Then there was a knock at the front door. When I opened it, there was a sweet Indian lady standing there. "Brother Duane," she said, "the Lord has been speaking to me for two weeks to bring you and your family some groceries... you have meant so much to my family and me...your messages have just changed our lives, and I just couldn't imagine you being in need...especially of food, and if I've missed God on this, please forgive me." As she kept going on and on with the apology, I just got to the point where I interrupted her and said, "Ma'am, you heard God loud and clear! Let's go get those groceries. We're starving!"

I learned so much through this trial of my faith. God had been speaking to this woman to give into the ministry for weeks and help provide for our family. God was continually working, moving, and speaking to people to give, and yet, they had to heed the lead and follow through with it as laborers together with Him. God uses people because it blesses them through their willing obedience in simple faith. He would have met my every need by bringing it to me on the wings of ravens had His people not responded, but He didn't want to bless a bird; He wanted to bless His people that love Him and are obedient to His call to serve others. As a result, she was excited beyond belief to have had the opportunity to serve us, and when she realized that she really had heard God and willingly obeyed Him, she grew immensely in her faith. At the same time, my faith soared when I saw that even when I couldn't see or feel it, God was diligently working on my behalf. For weeks God had been dealing with her (and I'm certain others) to sow and reap a harvest on good seeds sown.

My point in all this is that God is our faithful Husband, and He has already provided for all our needs according to His riches in glory. For Him to not take care of any one of us would mean that He has denied the faith, and it would reckon Him worse than an infidel. We, however, have the key that unlocks the door to this great and unending provision. It is through our simple faith in what He has already done for us at the cross (grace). Jesus has been the faithful provider that He promised to be, and this has caused great faith to be known and enjoyed generationally.

Jesus is not selfish. He truly loves us as Himself, and while we go through testing and trials, He is right there with us. He longs to be our all in all, the source and supply of every need we have. He wants to be our Healer, Deliverer, and Provider. *"But my God shall supply all your need according to his riches in glory by Christ Jesus"* (Philippians 4:19).

He wants us to *trust* Him and *look* to Him for every physical, soulical, and certainly spiritual need. He is jealous with godly jealousy when we look to the world to supply what only He can supply. The book of James makes some profound and challenging statements in this regard.

> *What is the cause of your conflicts and quarrels with each other? Doesn't the battle begin inside of you as you fight to have your own way and fulfill your own desires? You jealously want what others have so you begin to see yourself as better than others. You scheme with envy and harm others to selfishly obtain what you crave— that's why you quarrel and fight. And all the time you don't obtain what you want because* **you won't**

ask God for it! *And if you ask, you won't receive it for you're asking with corrupt motives, seeking only to ful-fill your own selfish desires. You have become* **spiritual adulterers who are having an affair, an unholy relationship with the world.** *Don't you know that flirting with the world's values places you at odds with God? Whoever chooses to be the world's friend makes himself God's enemy! Does the Scripture mean nothing to you that says, "The Spirit that God breathed into our hearts is a* **jealous Lover who intensely desires to have more and more of us**" (James 4:1-5 TPT).

Wow! He called us spiritual adulterers! Friendship with the world makes us an enemy of God. God is passionate toward us.

> Jesus wants us to leave the world as the source of our joy and other needs.

Jesus wants us to leave the world as the source of our joy and other needs. He wants us to cleave to Him as our steady focus, always receiving joy and peace, and living in His righteousness. God was jealous over Israel and wanted their affection and atten-tion as a husband does his wife. Jesus wants our affection and attention as well.

More than a Conqueror

No matter what we are facing, Jesus is faithful to us and declares us not *just* conquerors, but *more* than conquerors: *"Nay, in all these things we are more than conquerors through him that loved us"* (Romans 8:37).

When I met Sue, I was in college on a full-ride tennis scholarship and teaching tennis on the side. I played for the University of Central Florida and was phenomenally focused on my goal of becoming a professional tennis player. My dream was to go to Wimbledon and compete at the highest level in professional tennis, becoming one of the greatest players of the game. Of course, that all changed when the Lord told me that tennis had become a god in my life, and I was to put my racquet down.

SPIRITUAL AFFAIR

Tennis was, if you will, a competing lover with the Lord Himself. I was looking to tennis as the source of my identity, my future, and success in life. Tennis was my mistress with which the Lord was unwilling to compete. From that day forward, I gave myself wholly over to the work of the Kingdom and have never looked back. In fact, within two short years, I graduated from Bible college and was in full-time ministry.

While I have never regretted that decision, I've often contemplated the commitment and cost to not only make it to Wimbledon but to win it. The effort is almost unimaginable to most people. Friendships and relationships are replaced with countless hours on the court, hitting as many as 7,000 balls each week. Cross training, drills, instruction, and tournaments take up virtually every hour of every day while your thoughts are completely saturated with your game and how to improve it. Sweat, cramps, soreness, and pain become a normal part of your daily life in the relentless pursuit of winning the next match. Everything you do is affected by your focus to win the world championship.

ALTERNATE REALITY

These days it's hard for me to even imagine the joy of winning at Wimbledon and becoming one of tennis' greats, but let's just imagine a different scenario for a moment. Let's just say that God's face shined on me back in the day, and I had actually achieved my lofty goal. Let's pretend that all the work, all the pain, and all the dedication had finally paid off, and through great sacrifice and love for the game, I finally found myself standing before the Queen of England, receiving the trophy.

Wow—I'd made it! I imagine. *I was the winner of the greatest tournament in the game of tennis.* In my mind's eye, I can see her bowing to me as I stand before her. Wait a minute...another dyslexic moment. I graciously bow to the queen as she hands me a check for three million dollars. In that moment, I am a conqueror. I fulfilled my purpose and goal by conquest.

CONQUEROR VS. MORE THAN A CONQUEROR

But think about this: I go home and hand the check to Sue. She isn't a conqueror, she's *more* than a conqueror. She didn't lift a finger to win Wimbledon. She never endured the pain, the long arduous hours and sacrifice to perfect every stroke, or the mental strain and stress required to consistently perform at that level. Heck, she never even broke a sweat! Throughout the entire journey she never hit a tennis ball or even set foot on the court, yet she freely received that champion's purse. That's how it is between us and Jesus. Jesus is the husband with the trillion-dollar prize, and we are the recipients of His conquering and the proceeds from it. Blessings!

REALITY CHECK

In reality, I'm not a pro tennis player, and if I ever do end up going to Wimbledon it will be with a purchased ticket as a spectator, vicariously living my dream through the dedicated professionals on the court. But I want you to see that as a husband, I am the provider for my family. I'm created in the image and likeness of God *to work*, and it is in my divine design to provide for my wife and children. When payday comes, I get excited! When I look down at that paycheck, I see that I truly am a conqueror. I took on the challenges of the week, stayed focused and disciplined, and worked long, painstaking hours for that reward. I know in my heart that I've given my best effort to conquer the week's tasks. Now I have the compensation for that labor. But when I bring that check home and give it to Sue, she really gets excited because she's more than a conqueror. I earned the money by conquest, while she simply received the money by faith, freely reaping the blessing and benefit of my effort and sacrifice. That is a picture of being more than a conqueror.

> Jesus is the husband with the trillion-dollar prize, and we are the recipients of His conquering and the proceeds from it.

JESUS THE CONQUEROR

This is exactly how it is with our Husband, Jesus. All the pain, all the suffering, all the sacrifice that was made at the cross has paid the price for all the blessings we now have in this life and in the life to come. He achieved His goal when He conquered sin, hell, death, and the grave. He crushed the head of the serpent and spoiled all principalities and powers when He went to the cross. Jesus reinstated all the provision that the Father had intended for man from the beginning. All the promises of God in Him are yes, and they are printed on a check called the new covenant. He gives us all things freely to enjoy. He is indeed a conqueror, but we are now more than conquerors through Him that loved us. Because we are His wife, we now reap all the benefits of His life, labor, and love. By faith, we freely receive all the blessings that have been provided through His amazing grace. He is the best Provider the world has ever known or seen. He truly abounds toward us with all spiritual blessings, and we are only required to receive them by faith. That's what it means to be more than conquerors.

CHAPTER 9

KNOWING GOD

*These words spake Jesus, and lifted up his eyes to heaven, and said, Father, the hour is come; glorify thy Son, that thy Son also may glorify thee: As thou has given him power over all flesh, that he should give **eternal life** to as many as thou has given him. And this is **life eternal**, that they might **know thee** the only true God, and Jesus Christ whom thou has sent.*
—JOHN 17:1-3

Eternal life doesn't mean we will live forever. Everyone lives forever. We get to choose *where* we live forever. If we accept God's free gift of salvation by faith in Jesus, we live forever in His love, mercy, and kindness. If we reject His gift of salvation through unbelief, we live forever separated from His love, mercy, and kindness.

Eternal life is a quality of life (kind of life) not a quantity of life (number of years). Eternal life is knowing God, and this points to our personal relationship with Jesus by faith where there is a by-product (fruit). This word "know" from the Greek language was a Jewish idiom used specifically to define the intimate relationship between a husband and a wife that produces children. To know God is to have a personal relationship with Him where our spirits are united with Christ, and out of that spiritual union, we bear children (fruit) of the Kingdom. Galatians 5:22-23 calls these children the fruit of the Holy Spirit. They are "...*love, joy, peace, longsuffering, kindness, goodness, faithfulness gentleness, and self-control...*" (NKJV). All the positive changes in our lives are fruit. God's plan is that we bear much fruit and our fruit remain.

THE KJV NEW TESTAMENT GREEK LEXICON

Definition: *KNOW*

1. To learn to know, come to know, get a knowledge of, feel

2. To perceive, have knowledge, to understand, to become known

3. Jewish idiom for sexual intercourse between a man and a woman

Throughout the Old Testament, the word *know* in Hebrew is used regularly to define the intimacy that produced the fruit which built their legacy. It is always connected to the marriage relation between husband and wife, male and female as one flesh. Here are some examples where *know* is used: "*And Adam knew Eve his wife; and she conceived, and bare Cain, and said, I have gotten a man from the Lord*" (Genesis 4:1) "*And Cain knew his wife; and she conceived, and bare Enoch...*" (Genesis 4:17).

Can you see that a knowing is not very casual? It's not just a knowing *about,* but rather a knowing *of.* It is personal and intimate. *"And Adam knew his wife again; and she bare a son, and called his name Seth..."* (Genesis 4:25).

Notice this knowing is not a one-time event. "Adam knew his wife Eve again." They were growing in their knowing; it was an ongoing relationship producing children (fruit). Children are simply a by-product of a husband and wife knowing each other. Before marrying Isaac, Rebekah had kept herself pure and Scripture uses this same term: *"And the damsel was very fair to look upon, a virgin, neither had any man known her..."* (Genesis 24:16).

> Eternal life is knowing God, and this points to our personal relationship with Jesus by faith where there is a by-product (fruit).

Obviously, there were boys and men in her life that she knew or knew her in a casual kind of way. "No man having known" her is tied directly to her being a virgin, making it clear that this is speaking explicitly of a sexual relationship. This same meaning of the word *know* was used in the New Testament in the account of the angel Gabriel when he was sent from God to Mary to inform her of God's plans for her—to bring Emmanuel into this life. She was told she would have a baby and His name would be Jesus. *"Then said Mary unto the angel, How shall this be, seeing I know not a man?"* (Luke 1:34).

She knew she couldn't have a baby independent of physical intimacy with a husband. She had to choose to yield to the Holy Spirit and allow the supernatural conception to take place. Obviously, this is not just a casual acquaintance or polite handshake. This is a face-to-face relationship of intimacy that brings forth children (fruit). We, as the wife of Jesus, are to bring forth an abundance of fruit in the Kingdom of God. Our relationship with the Lord was never intended by God to be casual or just a knowledge about God. The only way we can bear fruit in the Kingdom is with an authentic closeness with the Lord. A personal relationship by faith in His pursuit of us in grace. One of the new covenant promises is, *"And they shall not teach every man his neighbor, and every man his brother, saying, Know the Lord: for all shall know me, from the least to the greatest"* (Hebrews 8:11).

All those who have accepted the new covenant (New Testament) have a promise that they can know the Lord Jesus Christ in an immediate, special, personal way. Out of this spiritual relationship with the Lord, we will bear much fruit. Jesus produces this life of abundance, and we, like a wife, bear the blessings. Marriage is not casual or distant. It's also not just a weekend-type of relationship.

> The only way we can bear fruit in the Kingdom is with an authentic closeness with the Lord.

Often people ask me, "Can you be saved and know it?"

I respond, "Can you get married and NOT know it?" Can you have a personal, intimate relationship with someone and not get pregnant? Everything changes at marriage including our marriage to Jesus. Eternal life is knowing God.

It is more than a knowing about God or a knowledge that is secondhand. This knowing has no mediators between us and God. When a husband knows his wife, children are a by-product. Through our knowledge of God, we bear the fruit of holiness (see Romans 6:22), and the fruit of the Spirit (see Galatians 5:22-23). All the fruit of the Christian life is *borne* by us (the wife), not produced. We can of our own selves do nothing. The Christian life is supernatural and simply comes out of our personal relationship with the Lord. For years I tried to please the Lord in my own self-effort and holiness. Struggling and striving to live this new life *for* Him but independent *of* Him. I finally came to a place of resting in His love for me and living from a place of faith in Him and complete dependence on Him. In other words, He produces this new life, and I by faith bear the fruit of it.

TEN VIRGINS (MATTHEW 25:1-12)

The parable of the ten virgins explains Christianity as a personal relationship with the Lord versus just religious works. The picture is that of a marriage relationship. Five of the virgins had oil and were considered wise; five had no oil and were called foolish. When the bridegroom arrived, the foolish could not borrow from the wise and were shut out of the marriage. When the five foolish asked to be let in, the Lord responded by saying, *"...I do not know you"* (Matthew 25:12 NKJV). *Knowing* here again means "intimate relationship." There is only one mediator between us and God and that is Jesus. Eternal life is knowing God through Jesus, His Son. We cannot be saved on other people's faith. We cannot bear fruit in the Kingdom of God independent of Jesus as our Husband and abiding in His Word.

THE DAY OF JUDGMENT

*A good tree can't produce bad fruit, and a bad tree can't produce good fruit. So every tree that does not produce good fruit is chopped down and thrown into the fire. Yes, just as you can identify a tree by its fruit, so you can identify people by their actions. "Not everyone who calls out to me, 'Lord! Lord!' will enter the Kingdom of Heaven. Only those who actually do the will of my Father in heaven will enter. On judgment day many will say to me, 'Lord! Lord! We prophesied in your name and cast out demons in your name and performed many miracles in your name.' But I will reply, '**I never knew you**. Get away from me, you who break God's laws'"* (Matthew 7:18-23 NLT)

On the day of judgment, many will think that their salvation is all about works. They will point to their works as the source of eternal life (salvation). The source of eternal life is knowing God (John 17:3) and, out of that relationship, comes good works (fruit). We are not saved *by* works, but rather *for* good works that come from knowing God. When our works (fruit) come from our love for God and a relationship of faith, that is pleasing to the Lord. When our works come from self, independent of God, to get Him to love us or bless us, that is not pleasing to the Lord. When Jesus said, "I never knew you," He was saying there was not a relationship of grace and faith. There was no husband and wife relationship where all our works (fruit) are a by-product of our love and faith relationship. There is nothing wrong with good works, and they are very much a part of our newfound life in

Jesus, but where do they come from? They must come from knowing God (eternal life) and having a relationship with Him. Pure Christianity is all about relationship, not religion.

ONLY ONE VIRGIN BIRTH

Over the years, Sue and I have prayed for literally hundreds of couples to conceive and have children. Sometimes the physical problem was on the husband's end, and other times, it was the wife who could not carry a child. Regardless of the natural circumstances, the truth of God's Word always trumps the facts of this life. Because we know that, we have seen the goodness of God miraculously manifest when, in the natural, there was no hope at all. We've personally seen miracle after miracle with couples who have believed the promises that God has given them in spite of their circumstances.

> Pure Christianity is all about relationship, not religion.

Years ago, at the end of one of my meetings, I was praying for people in a long line when one unforgettable woman approached. When I asked her what she needed prayer for she said, "I've heard testimonies of you praying for people to have a baby and the miracles that have happened, and I want you to pray for me to have a baby."

Because we are so passionate about this, I immediately answered her, "Absolutely, I will pray for you to have a baby!" Then I asked if her husband was present at the service so that he could stand in agreement with her. There's no greater covenant bond in prayer than that of a husband and a wife standing in agreement together with Jesus in the middle; the Bible tells us that *"a three-fold cord is not quickly broken"* (Ecclesiastes 4:12). I emphasized that Sue and I have seen many miracles in this area, and that I absolutely believed it is because we join together, praying with both the husband and the wife and that our unity in prayer overcomes anything that is physically wrong or hindering God's will for a couple to bear children. We believe without wavering that children are a heritage of the Lord, and the fruit of the womb is His reward. We are commanded in Genesis 1:28 to be fruitful and replenish the earth. If you want a baby; God wills for you to have one.

After me trying to encourage her in regard to her husband so that we could pray for him as well, she said, "I don't have a husband." At first, I thought there had to be some misunderstanding concerning her request. She was asking to have a baby, and everyone knows that it's just "not happenin'" without a husband. I apologized and asked her a second time what her prayer request was, certain that I had misheard her. She said a second time without hesitation, "I want to have a baby!" Good or bad, my personality is a little twisted, and there are times that words just seem to slip right out of my mouth when I'm caught off guard. So I said to her, "Ma'am, I could lay hands on you till you're bald, but without a husband, you will not conceive and have a baby!"

Now I'll give her credit for believing the scripture that says with God all things are possible but that's within the confines of His Word and His will. There's only been one virgin birth in this earth, and there will never be another because there will never be a need for another. God established procreation in the garden with Adam and Eve where the two become one flesh and through that intimacy produce and bear children that fill the earth with His glory. Yet somehow, she believed that just through me praying for her that she could get pregnant and have a baby. What I had to lovingly explain to her was that she needed to get married and let her husband lay hands on her; that's how it works!

I certainly hope that this story sounds as crazy to you as it did to me. I really couldn't wrap my mind around anyone thinking that they could actually conceive and bear children independent of an intimate relationship with a spouse. Then I thought about how many believers in the Church are living their lives every day, thinking they can bear fruit independent of an intimate relationship with their spiritual Husband, Jesus. We never produce the fruit in our own lives, we only bear it. Like husbands that carry the seed to fertilize the egg of the wife, Jesus is the promised seed that fertilizes and produces the Kingdom "offspring" in our lives. No woman is able to get pregnant without the seed of the man, and no believer will ever bear Kingdom fruit without the seed of the bridegroom, the Living Word of God. Consider Jesus' words to us in this regard:

> *I am the true vine, and My Father is the vinedresser. Every branch in Me that does not **bear fruit** He takes away; and every branch that **bears fruit** He prunes, that it may **bear** more fruit. You are already clean because of the word which I have spoken to you. Abide in Me, and I in you. As the branch cannot **bear fruit** of itself, unless it abides in the vine, neither can you, unless you abide in Me. I am the vine you are the branches. He who abides in Me, and I in him, **bears***

much fruit; for without Me you can do nothing (John 15:1-5 NKJV).

Jesus said that without Him you can do nothing. It's in abiding (relational terms) that we bear much fruit. We are to be yoked to Jesus, ever learning of Him and continually developing our husband-wife relationship. Just like the Holy Spirit overshadowed the promised Seed (Jesus) in a teenage girl named Mary, we too need to allow the Holy Spirit to overshadow the Word of God that is sown into our hearts. When we do, we will bear Kingdom offspring within us and without, which will bring life to a lost and dying world. A Christian trying to live this new life and bear the fruit of the Kingdom independent of Jesus and His Word should be as strange to us as the story of that precious lady who was trying to have children without a husband.

> We are to be yoked to Jesus, ever learning of Him and continually developing our husband-wife relationship.

GOD'S WORD IS SEED

All seed has life inside to reproduce after its own kind. It must be sown into good ground and then harvested in order to be beneficial and enjoyed. God's Word is like seed with the power in it to reproduce after its own kind if sown into a heart that is good ground. Jesus taught on God's Word as seed and is one of the most important parables He ever taught.

*He taught them by telling many stories in the form of parables, such as this one: "Listen! A farmer went out to plant some seed. As he scattered it across his field, some of the seed fell on a footpath, and the birds came and ate it. Other seed fell on shallow soil with underlying rock. The seed sprouted quickly because the soil was shallow. But the plant soon wilted under the hot sun, and since it didn't have deep roots, it died. Other seed fell among thorns that grew up and choked out the tender plants so they produced no grain. Still other seeds fell on fertile soil, and they sprouted, grew, and produced a crop that was thirty, sixty, and even a hundred times as much as had been planted!" Then he said, "Anyone with ears to hear should listen and **understand**"* (Mark 4:2-9 NLT).

Mark 4:13-20 is the explanation of the parable of the farmer who scatters seed. There are different types of ground that seed is sown in that brings different degrees of a harvest. This is one of the most important parables in all of Scripture. Jesus declared in verse 13 that if we don't understand this parable, we will struggle with every other parable. He said, *"...If you can't understand the meaning of this parable, how will you understand all the other parables? The farmer plants seed by taking God's word to others"* (Mark 4:13-14 NLT).

The farmers are those who share God's Word with others. God's Word is described as seed. Just like natural seeds must be sown in the earth to release the life and power within the seed to produce fruit, God's Word is spiritual seed that must be sown in our hearts to produce the fruit of a changed heart and a new life.

First Ground (Heart)

"*The seed that fell on the footpath represents those who hear the message, only to have Satan come at once and take it away*" (Mark 4:15 NLT). Notice that Satan wants to steal God's Word (seed) to keep us fruitless. Mark did not explain how Satan does it, but Matthew's account of this parable does. "*The seed that fell on the footpath represents those who hear the message about the Kingdom and don't understand it. Then the evil one comes and snatches away the seed that was planted in their hearts*" (Matthew 13:19 NLT).

Satan can steal the Word when we don't understand what God is saying to us. As we pursue God and persist in our relationship with Him, the Holy Spirit gives us the understanding and fruit will come. Revelation knowledge is God's Word (seed) taking root in our hearts in understanding; we hear what God says, know what He means and how to apply it to our lives.

Second Ground (Heart)

> The seed on rocky soil represents those who hear the message and immediately receive it with joy. But since **they don't have deep roots** they don't last long. They fall away as soon as they have **problems** or are **persecuted** for believing God's word (Mark 4:16-17 NLT).

All problems and persecutions are designed by Satan to remove God's Word from our hearts. Why? Because it is the Word (seed) that produces fruit. It's abiding in Jesus that we get rooted and grounded in Him (Colossians 2:6-7). Allowing Him to lead us through sufferings lets the Word (seed) change us and our circumstances.

Third Ground (Heart)

*The seed that fell among the thorns represents others who hear God's word, but all too quickly the message is crowded out by the **worries** of this life, the **lure of wealth**, and the **desire for other things**, so no fruit is produced* (Mark 4:18-19 NLT).

These three common distractions are deadly, daily forces that make God's Word of no effect. While an entire book can be written on the three things that choke God's Word in our lives, the real issue here is how it is only God's Word that makes the difference. As powerful as God's Word is, it cannot overrule the negative effect of these three. Worry, the lure of wealth, and desire for other things choke the Word in our hearts and limit its potential. Many good

> Our lives being changed and transformed is all about how we relate to the seed of God's Word.

people wonder why God's Word isn't working for them. Usually it comes back to these three things. As we choose to guard our hearts in these areas, God's Word will take root, and in time, we will bear much fruit.

Fourth Ground (Heart)

*And the seed that fell on **good soil** represents those who **hear and accept God's word** and produce a harvest of* *thirty, sixty, or even a hundred times as much as had been planted!* (Mark 4:20 NLT).

Our lives being changed and transformed is all about how we relate to the seed of God's Word. Our hearts are the womb where God's seed is sown. All of us as the wife of Jesus have a spiritual womb. (Men, remember we must think role (wife), not gender). One of the Greek words for seed is *sperma* (Matthew 13:24), which is where we get our English word "sperm." Just like the sperm of a husband produces life in the womb of his wife and she bears fruit (children), the Word of God sown into our hearts (spiritual womb) will produce change and fruit in our lives if we guard our hearts with all diligence. We can have a relationship with God where we hear His Word, receive it in our hearts, and with it, produce a new life in Christ. We've been born again by the seed of God's Word (1 Peter 1:23) and by this new life have overcome the world. This principle is a huge part of the mystery of Christ and the Church.

> When we are born again of God's seed, we are no longer victims but now victors.

As the bride of Jesus, we are called "world overcomers" (1 John 5:4-5). When we are born again of God's seed, we are no longer victims but now victors. While we all face obstacles daily in this life, we are fighting *from* a position of victory, not *for* victory. As Jesus' wife, we already have been declared the winners in every battle. We all have opportunities to feel discouraged in life and may say things like: "That promotion has evaded me now three times." "It looks like I'm the loser in life's lottery." "No one recognizes my gifts and value." Seedtime and harvest are immutable laws. If you will believe God's Word and put it in your heart and if you will speak God's Word in praise and thanksgiving out of your mouth, your harvest will come as sure as the sun rises and sets. You're not just a normal man or woman. You're the bride of Jesus, and greater is He that is in you than he that is in the world. You can no longer claim victim status as the bride of Jesus. *You married into victory!*

CHAPTER 10

LAW OF JEALOUSY

*Thus says the Lord of host: I am Jealous for
Zion with great jealousy and I am Jealous
with great wrath [against her enemies].*
—ZECHARIAH 8:2 AMPC

They say that jealousy makes you nasty and ugly. When out of balance, human jealousy does, indeed, bring out the worse in us all. But there is nothing nasty or ugly about the jealousy our heavenly Husband has for us, because Jesus is jealous over us with godly jealousy. It is both a pure and beautiful concept that few have considered.

In return, He desires our full attention and our passion. He has an intense love for us. He pursues us and wants us to respond in faith. He wants total dependency on Him in all things that pertain to this life and eternity. Total reliance on Him as our Husband is what pleases Him greatly.

Many things in our world are competing for our attention and our worship. Many of us are married to a job or career, a doctrine, rules and regulations, or a political party just to mention a few. Think of the passion and commitment that people have for these things, yet so little for Jesus. The Lord taught us that, *"If you want to be my disciple, you must, by comparison, hate everyone else—your father and mother, wife and children, brothers and sisters—yes, even your own life. Otherwise, you cannot be my disciple"* (Luke 14:26 NLT).

> Being a disciple (a disciplined follower) is actually learning to become a mature bride to the Lord.

Being a disciple (a disciplined follower) is actually learning to become a mature bride to the Lord. It's not that we have no affection for these other things, but by comparison to our love for Jesus, the others should pale greatly.

SCRIPTURES POINT TO A PERSON

You search the Scriptures because you think they give you eternal life. **But the Scriptures point to me!** *Yet you refuse to* **come to me** *to receive this life* (John 5:39-40 NLT).

Even as important as the Scriptures are to us, we can't be married to a book either. We are married to a *Person*. When people yoke themselves to the letter of Scripture versus the Spirit, they lose their passion and zeal for God as well as their peace and joy; it brings death (2 Corinthians 3:6). However, being yoked to the

Author of the Book brings invigorating life and joy unspeakable and full of glory. Over the years, I've met people who know what the Bible says but somehow missed the Author and overarching theme of the Bible. Rather than using the Word to love people, they are actually abusive with it.

The Scriptures *reveal* Jesus, they do not *replace* Him. The Scriptures lead us *to* Him, not away from Him. The Word of God is like a menu. It testifies of something bigger and greater than itself. Think of it like a person sitting in a restaurant studying the menu. They could memorize it, quote it, and dance with it to the jukebox music, but if they don't order, they will starve and die! The Scriptures are the *menu* and Jesus is the *meal*. We must mix faith with the Word of God and get past the letter and understand the Spirit of the Word, Jesus. It is the only way it will benefit us. Hebrews 4:2 expresses this point beautifully: *"...but the word which they heard did not profit them, not being mixed with faith in those who heard it"* (NKJV).

The combination of grace and faith brings life. Grace is God's part, and faith is ours. With the Word, Jesus abounds toward us in grace, and we respond in the action of faith. Jesus' godly jealousy demands a response in faith. The Word only profits us when we act on it in faith. Many people sit in church and die spiritually because they are "wed" to something besides Jesus. Please don't misunderstand me, God's Word is the most important thing in my life. It has created hope and desire in my heart for all the precious attributes and blessings that God has for me. *"For all the promises of God in him are yea, and in him Amen, unto the glory of God by us"* (2 Corinthians 1:20).

All the promises of God that are found in the menu of the Scriptures are in Jesus, and all the promises in that menu are yes and amen for us. It brings God glory when we experience all the rich benefits Jesus has provided. It is our devoted response to our loving husband in receiving and walking in all His promises.

DEVOTION TO JESUS

*For I am **jealous** for you with the **jealousy of God himself**. I promised you as a pure bride to one husband—Christ. But I fear that somehow your **pure and undivided devotion to Christ** will be corrupted, just as Eve was deceived by the cunning ways of the serpent* (2 Corinthians 11:2-3 NLT).

Like any husband, Jesus' jealousy is directly connected to our response to Him and our commitment to remaining faithful. Paul feared that just as Satan deceived Eve, the people would also be corrupted in their minds from the simplicity of their focus on Christ. God doesn't want us (the wife of Jesus) to be deceived and drawn away from Him. As His bride, Jesus tells us what is right and wrong, good or evil, moral or immoral. How many in today's culture have had their minds corrupted from the simplicity of these things? When we are disloyal to our Husband Jesus, we are easily deceived. God doesn't want to complicate things in our lives. He has made it very simple. He desires a love relationship. Period. He points us to building, developing, and growing in our love with and for the Lord. That means loving Him more than what He provides and more than all the many blessings and benefits. Jesus longs for us to love Him more than all the cheap counterfeits Satan and the world can supply. If it's not good things or even God things drawing us away, then it's the hardships and challenges of this life. All the trials, tribulation, and afflictions of everyday life can tug us away from the Lord if they are not properly understood and approached in simplicity and in faith.

HARDSHIPS IN LIFE

Early in our marriage, Sue and I learned that in hardship it was best for us to pull close to each other and turn to God in unison. This forged a great trust and bond of friendship. All the problems in life are designed by Satan to separate us from the love Jesus has for us (Romans 8) and to undermine our response and our faithfulness toward Him. You and I need to be convinced that nothing can separate us from the love of God in Jesus. When things come against us (and they will), we need to develop the "run to God" mindset. Instead of doubting or falsely

> Jesus longs for us to love Him more than all the cheap counterfeits Satan and the world can supply.

accusing the Lord of causing the trouble, we need to forge an ever-greater bond of friendship and companionship as seen here: *"Submit yourselves therefore to God. Resist the devil, and he will flee from you. Draw nigh to God, and he will draw nigh to you..."* (James 4:7-8).

Throughout my time in ministry, I have always been perplexed at how easily people give up on Jesus and how quick they are to blame Him for the bad things that happen in life. We live in a dark, fallen world, and while we've been delivered from the *powers of darkness* (Colossians 1:13), we have not been delivered from the *presence* of darkness. Bad things happen to good people. Bad stuff is all around us. When bad things happen, most people get hung up on the issue of God's role in them versus Satan's. They are quick to think things like, *God must be doing this to punish me for sin* or *God is doing this to teach me something.* They often assign blame to God and miss how Satan's primary goal is to separate us from God through all these trials and tribulations. In assuming the trial was caused by God instead of Satan, they push away God and miss the blessings of a deeper relationship with Jesus.

When trials come, don't allow Satan to deceive you into believing that Jesus, your Husband, has wavered in His love and commitment to you. Do not even entertain the suspicion that His will for you as His wife is calamity of any form. His will for His wife is nothing less than to thrive and bloom into your greatest potential. Notice how James, the brother of Jesus, explains this: *"So don't be misled, my dear brothers and sisters. Whatever is good and perfect is a gift coming down to us from God our Father, who created all the lights in the heavens. He never changes or casts a shifting shadow"* (James 1:16-17 NLT).

Many Christians have been taught things about God that are blatantly untrue. I'm not sure where some of the false teachings originated. Maybe people are yoked up with a different Jesus than the One I know—the Jesus of the Bible. Perhaps their experience with an abusive father or husband has damaged their view of what a godly husband looks like. I don't know how the Church at large became so muddled in this subject. What I do know is that God desires to renew our minds and show us the true image of a husband in the person of Jesus. That image is one of love for you and God's best for you in every area of life.

GOD GOOD—DEVIL BAD

Because of the widespread confusion in this area, I'd like to take this principle down to brass tacks: God good. Devil bad. It really is that simple. God has no ill will for you. Period. The devil has only ill will for you. Period. God has nothing but good gifts. The devil has nothing but bad. If it's not a good gift, then it's not from God. If it's postmarked "from above," it is a good gift. If it's a bad gift then, "return to sender." Cancer is not a good gift. It is not from God, so refuse to receive it. Poverty, sickness, strife, confusion—NOTHING that hurts us is from Him.

Would a good husband put any disease on his wife? Would he want poverty, lack, or sickness for her? Would a good husband abuse his wife to teach her something or leave her alone in times of distress or grief? Absolutely NOT. Well, you are the wife of Jesus. You are His beloved bride. Just keep rolling that over in your head. His will is nothing but good for you. He only desires to see you happy, healthy, and successful in life. "*The thief's purpose is to steal and kill and destroy. My purpose is to give them a rich and satisfying life*" (John 10:10 NLT).

WORKING FOR GOOD

*And we know that all things work together **for good** to them that **love God**, to them who are the called according to **his purpose*** (Romans 8:28).

All things are not good or of God in this life, so this is a profound promise that God will work all things together for our good; and that it is conditional on us loving God and being called according to His purpose, not our own. What an over-the-top promise! What a blessing to have a husband so committed to our success and happiness in life. Viewing life through our union with Christ can change how trials and afflictions can be perceived. They are not a test of God's love and faithfulness to His wife, but rather a test of the Church's, His wife's, love and faithfulness to Him.

I discovered this plain truth in Numbers 5, in what Moses called the "law of jealousy." This chapter outlines the process of testing a wife's faithfulness to her husband. If you are an avid Bible student, and you enjoy reading Levitical law, I am referring to Numbers 5:11-31 and I encourage you to read through this portion of scripture. But for those of you whose Bible reading plans seem to avoid books like Leviticus and Numbers, I have paraphrased this section of scripture for you.

The law of jealousy goes something like this (see Numbers 5:11-31): Under the Mosaic law, if a husband became jealous and suspicious of his wife and thought that she had perhaps had an affair, he could take his wife to the priest to identify if she was in fact faithful or not. The husband had to take along a special offering to invoke the test. The priest would mix some holy water with the dust from the temple floor creating a mixture of "bitter water" which was placed in a jar or cup for her to drink. Before the test started, the priest would explain the proceedings to the woman. She was to drink the cup, and if she was guilty, she would become infertile. Her womb would shrivel, her abdomen swell, and all would know that she was cursed because of her unfaithfulness. If she was not guilty, then the bitter water would have no effect on her. She would live free from the bitter cup and go on to conceive children with her husband. Once the woman agreed by saying the words "let it be so," the test began. There would be no repercussions for the husband whatever the results of the test, but the wife would be held fully accountable if the bitter water demonstrated her guilt.

I agree with you if you are thinking that this seems pretty bizarre! Before I understood the "great mystery," these passages were confusing and complicated. In many ways, they seemed unequitable in the marriage relation. The husband could have her tested with no evidence at all but rather on suspicion alone. Why was only the wife's faithfulness tested and not that of the husband also? When I applied the concepts of the "great mystery," it then made perfect sense. Since husbands are a type of Christ and wives the Church (see Ephesians 5:32), I put Christ in place of the husband and us, the Church, in place of the wife. Like all Scripture, we have need of the Holy Spirit to reveal God's heart, but these were among the most difficult for me. I'm sure I've not seen all God has from the law of jealousy, but what I have seen has been valuable and precious. Here are a few truths God has revealed:

1. The husband could not be tested for his faithfulness.

How unfair is that?! It seems like a rotten deal. There was no reciprocal law where the wife could have the husband tested. His sole criteria was to be willing to bring and offer a sacrifice. The only way this could be just and right is if the husband is a type of Christ. Remember, it was the husband who brought an offering for his wife's alleged sin (see Numbers 5:15). Jesus, our Husband, did not offer an offering for our sin, but rather *became* the offering for our sins. Jesus and His love for us was demonstrated at the cross, and guess what? He passed the test. *"But God commendeth his love toward us, in that, while we were yet sinners, Christ died for us"* (Romans 5:8).

The Lord's love for me was put to the ultimate test, and He passed with flying colors. His love and faithfulness to me is never under question. He has proven His love for me in the work of the cross. When I hear a voice saying, "If God loved you, why is this happening to you?" I can cast down those thoughts immediately with confidence. It is not God's love for me that is on trial; it is my love for God.

2. Bitter cups are Christian sufferings.

In the testing of the wife's faithfulness, the priest would take a clay jar or cup and put holy water mixed with dust from the temple floor into it (see Numbers 5:17). Really? Dust from the temple floor! Can you imagine how filthy that floor was from the foot traffic that came from the fields plus all the blood shed from the sacrifices? Let's just say it was all kinds of nasty. I can't imagine how "bitter" that cup became, and the thought of drinking it nauseates me. I guess the real test was if the wife would even drink it.

> The Lord's love for me was put to the ultimate test, and He passed with flying colors.

If she refused to drink it, she would be seen as guilty in the refusal. The illustration here is that all of our trials are bitter cups and a test of our love and faithfulness to Jesus. Jesus spoke of a cup in this manner. He used cups and the drinking of a cup as it relates to sufferings. *"He went on a little farther and bowed with his face to the ground, praying, 'My Father! If it is possible, let this cup of suffering be taken away from me. Yet I want your will to be done, not mine.' ... Then Jesus left them a second time and prayed, 'My Father! If this cup cannot be taken away unless I drink it, your will be done'"* (Matthew 26:39, 42 NLT).

On the cross, Jesus drank of a cup of suffering for us that cannot be imagined. He endured unspeakable agony and paid the ultimate penalty for all our sins. I'm so thankful He was willing to drink that cup. How did He manage it? He kept His focus on His unfathomable love for us. No bitter cup that we may have to drink can be remotely compared to the cup He drank on our behalf. The way we drink them is out of our love and faithfulness to Him.

MOMS WILL BE MOMS

*Then the mother of James and John, the sons of Zebedee, came to Jesus with her sons. She knelt respectfully to ask a favor. "What is your request?" he asked. She replied, "In your Kingdom, please let my two sons sit in places of honor next to you, one on your right and the other on your left." But Jesus answered by saying to them, "You don't know what you are asking! Are you able to **drink from the bitter cup of suffering** I am about to drink?" "Oh yes," they replied, "we are able!" Jesus told them, "**You will indeed drink from my bitter cup**. But I have no right to say who will sit on my right or my left. My Father has prepared those* *places for the ones he has chosen"* (Matthew 20:20-23 NLT).

This over-zealous mother really had no idea what she was asking. You would think having two boys on the "Big Twelve Team" (twelve apostles) would have been enough. I guess moms will be moms. She wants one boy on the left, the other on the right of Jesus in His Kingdom. Jesus asked them if they could drink from the bitter cup of suffering that He would drink. They assured Him that they could. Jesus said that they would indeed drink from His bitter cup. In other words, we would all share in the sufferings of Christ. We would enter into a matrimonial partnership where we fellowship in the same sufferings: persecution for being godly (2 Timothy 3:12) and being hated and even killed for His name's sake (Matthew 10:22, Matthew 24:9).

The apostle Paul makes reference to these bitter cups. *"Yea doubtless, and I count all things but loss for the excellency of the knowledge of Christ Jesus my Lord: for whom I have suffered the loss of all things, and do count them but dung, that I may win Christ, And be found in him, not having mine own righteousness, which is of the law, but that which is through the faith of Christ, the righteousness which is of God by faith: That I may know him and the power of his resurrection, and the fellowship of his sufferings, being made conformable unto his death"* (Philippians 3:8-10). In Romans 8:17-18 a reference to godly suffering is mentioned but also a promise of what follows the sufferings: *"And if children, then heirs; heirs of God, and joint-heirs with Christ; if so be that we suffer with him, that we may be also glorified together. For I reckon that the sufferings of this present time are not worthy to be compared with the glory which shall be revealed in us."*

Although there are forms of suffering associated with the new life of Christ in us, no suffering is worthy to be compared to the glory that shall be revealed in us. At the appearing of Jesus and His Kingdom, we will shine with the glory of God in us as the stars of heaven. Notice it will be revealed in us, not to us. The glory is in us, in Christ, in our spirit man. Through the new birth and the new creation, our spirit man is united to Christ as one spirit now (see 1 Corinthians 6:17).

All the trials and tribulations of the Christian are shared by Jesus, our Husband. It's never Him putting bad things on us but Jesus fellowshipping, encouraging, and strengthening us through the hardships of life.

In the next chapter, we will look at "bitter cups" and how to deal with them in our faithfulness to Jesus. We will also break down all the types and shadows of Numbers 5 as it relates to our marriage to Jesus.

CHAPTER 11

BITTER CUPS

Let's do a quick review of the concept of bitter cups because this is new to most believers. The law of jealousy in Numbers 5:11-31 is where we see the husband's wife being tested for her faithfulness. Within the testing process was a "bitter cup" she had to drink before the Lord (Numbers 5:18-19). There were consequences if she was unfaithful to her husband and a blessing if she endured the test. Jesus used bitter cups as a reference to Christian suffering. There are observations and wisdom that come from this "law of jealousy."

OBSERVATION #1: THE HUSBAND COULD NOT BE TESTED FOR HIS FAITHFULNESS.

Jesus is perfect in His faithfulness. There can be no doubt about Jesus' faithfulness to us when we consider what He went through at the cross. All trials, afflictions, tribulations, and persecutions are a test of our love and faithfulness to our husband Jesus, not God's love for us. Remember every trial is a test. Had it been an actual emergency Jesus would have come back! We pass the test by staying faithful to Jesus, not blaming Him or no longer serving Him because "it's just too hard."

OBSERVATION #2: BITTER CUPS ARE CHRISTIAN SUFFERINGS.

Jesus called the suffering of the cross a "cup of suffering" (Matthew 26:39-42). There are multiple witnesses in regard to Christian sufferings in the New Testament. The apostle Peter speaks of a kind of suffering that is scriptural. *"Beloved, think it not strange concerning the fiery trial which is to try you, as though some strange thing happened unto you: But rejoice, inasmuch as ye are partakers of Christ's sufferings; that, when his glory shall be revealed, ye may be glad also with exceeding joy. If ye be reproached for the name of Christ, happy are ye; for the spirit of glory and of God resteth upon you: on their part he is evil spoken of but on your part he is glorified. But let none of you suffer as a murderer, or as a thief, or as an evil-doer, or as a busybody in other men's matters. Yet if any man suffers as a Christian, let him not be ashamed; but let him glorify God on this behalf"* (1 Peter 4:12-16).

When fiery trials come, don't think that something strange has happened. They definitely will come, so be prepared—not perplexed. While some suffering is a result of poor judgment or choices that don't please God, there is a spectrum of Christian suffering that should not make us feel shameful. There is suffering wrongfully for doing the right thing, suffering mockery because of our desire for purity and holiness, being hated because we love what God loves, being rejected by our families for our faith in Jesus, believing in God's Word above all others, and even being martyred because of our faith. Suffering is a difficult subject for so many, and they wonder how to tell what things are God's will that we suffer and what are not.

Jesus suffered many things on our behalf as a "substitute," so we wouldn't have to suffer them. Our sins, sickness, poverty, etc. were taken by Him on the cross. There are many other things that Jesus suffered as an "example" for us to

> There can be no doubt about Jesus' faithfulness to us when we consider what He went through at the cross.

follow: persecution, tribulations, rejection, being hated for doing good, etc. We must remain faithful as these different bitter cups come even though we hear Satan whisper things like:

- "If God loves you, why did your baby die?"
- "If God loves you, why did you get cancer?"
- "If God loves you, why are you divorced?"

Just remember God's love for you is not on trial; your love for Him is. Remain faithful and watch Him work all things together for your good and bring Him glory.

OBSERVATION #3: WHAT IF SHE WAS UNFAITHFUL?

What if the wife in Numbers 5 had been unfaithful to her husband? If the wife was unfaithful, she would come under a three-fold curse. Her womb would shrivel, her abdomen would swell, and her name would be a curse among her people. She would be childless or in other words, "bear no fruit" (Numbers 5:21-28). It is very important to note here that we are no longer under any curse of the law. Christ has totally and completely redeemed us from it all. *"Christ hath redeemed us from the curse of the law, being made a curse for us: for it is written, cursed is every one that hangeth on a tree"* (Galatians 3:13).

While we are no longer under any curse associated with the law, we are not exempt from the consequences of sin. All sin brings unintended consequences into our lives and the lives of those around us. If we yield to sin, Satan can use it to steal, kill, and destroy us. Through sin, we've given him an inroad to hinder and damage all of the wonderful things God's grace has afforded us (see Romans 6:16, John 10:10). Again, I want to stress that we are no longer under any curse, but there are consequences for unfaithfulness. There are still wages—not God's wrath—to sin in our lives. The law of sowing and reaping was not rendered null and void by the cross. We are warned in Galatians 6 of sowing to the flesh rather than the Spirit. Unfaithfulness to Jesus in the bitter cups of life have consequences. Let's examine the three that Moses mentions:

"Her womb would shrivel"—Numbers 5:21

Christ loves nothing more than when we are fruitful. Bearing fruit in our lives means that the Kingdom is bearing fruit, which excites our Husband, Jesus. But fruitfulness only comes from faithfully abiding in Jesus and allowing Him to abide in us (see John 15). When we are unfaithful to Him, our "womb" (the womb of our hearts) shrinks and we cease bearing fruit. The lack of fruit in our lives is not God punishing us, but sin and Satan robbing us.

We must remain faithful to Jesus in the trials of this life (bitter cups) and not draw back or falsely accuse Him. Being infertile was never God's will or plan for the Church. It is unfaithfulness to Jesus and His Word that creates barrenness in the Kingdom.

"Her abdomen would swell" —Numbers 5:21

Because of her unfaithfulness to her husband, the bitter waters of the cup would get inside of her. The bitterness would cause her belly to swell. Hebrews 12:15 warns us of a root of bitterness springing up in many of God's people and defiling them. People who run away from Jesus in times of trial have swollen bellies. We know that because when bitterness is inside of us it defiles our words with murmuring and complaining. Trials, if responded to properly in our relationship and fellowship with Jesus, can make us *better* people. If we are unfaithful in the hardships of life, we become *bitter* people.

"Her name would be a curse among her people..." —Numbers 5:27

When we spend our time complaining, it affects our closeness with the Lord and that affects everyone around us. A person who consistently complains is not a blessing among their people. Think about the people who light up a room when they walk in. Do they have a habit of murmuring and complaining, or do they make everyone in the room feel special, appreciated and loved? That's because they do not have a root of bitterness on the inside of them. I can say that, while I love all of God's people, I have a hard time being around fruitless, bellyaching people. I much prefer the company of fruit-bearing, encouraging friends who stay far away from bitterness. I know I want to light up a room when I walk in, not out. Don't be that guy.

OBSERVATION #4: WHAT IF SHE WAS FAITHFUL?

If the wife was faithful, she would be free from the curse and the bitter water. There would be no negative side effects to the drinking of the bitter cup. She then would be able to have children. It's been my consistent witness and experience that it is often after a fiery trial that we bear new fruit. We simply need to learn to drink the cup and move on to the fruit part. I'm not going to avoid the bitter cup or sip it like a little baby with a sippy cup, complaining about how unfair life is. When I say drink and move on, I'm not saying we just cave and give in to problems; no, quite the contrary. I'm saying I love Jesus, and nothing will separate me from Him. I've been faithful and I will remain so, and that bitter cup will pass with no ill effects. I've had bitter cups rock my world, but drawing close to Jesus, has caused me to conceive in the womb of my heart and bring forth much fruit that glorifies the Father (John 15:8).

So many good people believe that faith is all about problem avoidance. They think, *If we just had more faith, we wouldn't have these problems.* Try telling that to the apostle Paul. He and Jesus both warned us of impending tribulation and persecution in this life. Notice how Jesus instructs us to face and deal with the impending trials and tribulations of life (bitter cups). *"These things I have spoken unto you, that in me ye might have peace. In the world ye shall have tribulation: but be of good cheer; I have overcome the world"* (John 16:33).

Paul understood these things as well. Notice his words from Acts 14:22; *"...we must through much tribulation enter into the kingdom of God."* As we enter into God's Kingdom (His rule and reign in our life), there will be opposition. Temptations to quit or give up on the good fight of faith are knocking on the door of our heart constantly. I recommend not opening the door!

Be of good cheer? Really? Come on, man. That's not real! Without faith in God and knowing His commitment to me in my sufferings, I would agree. He is not only faithful to me, but also, I can by faith be of good cheer because He overcame the world. I used to read that and think: *Good for you Jesus, but what about me?* His victory over the world was for me. He conquered the world as my Husband, and He's making me more than a conqueror through Him as His wife. Wow! What a blessing! *"Yea, and all that will live godly in Christ Jesus shall suffer persecution"* (2 Timothy 3:12).

> Temptations to quit or give up on the good fight of faith are knocking on the door of our heart constantly. I recommend not opening the door!

Before reading the next sentence, pause and say, "I love Brother Duane." If you're not suffering some form of persecution, it's because you are not living very godly. I know that's very direct, but it is also very true. Again, the real test for the wife was in her willingness. If she was unwilling to drink the cup, she was guilty by appearance. How many innocent women under that law of jealousy had to go through that test? I can't be the only one who has thought, *What have I done to deserve this test? Why is this happening to me? I deserve better than this. Is this what I get for serving God?*

Can you imagine all the spiritual warfare raging in the wife's mind just by being escorted to the temple to see the preacher?! When I was an immature bride, I struggled, but I have come to understand it's all about faithfulness. Just drink the cup, draw nigh to your Husband as a partaker of His sufferings, and fellowship with Him, knowing He will work it all together for good.

I'm not in this marriage for the fishes and loaves. I'm in it because of the love I've seen in Jesus for us; I'm in such a partnership that these bitter cups are merely causing strength in our relationship, not weakening it.

AN UNTIMELY DEATH

In the fall of 1976, I picked up a tennis racket and started hitting some balls, beginning my tennis career. A coach saw talent in me, so I worked hard at it and ended up number one on the team in my senior year. My younger brother, Jimmy, had just come off house arrest from the authorities and had been given permission to go out with some friends. He begged me to go with him, but because I had a tennis tournament early the next morning, I felt it best to keep my focus and stay home. Later that night the dreaded knock came on our door. It was the police. My brother had been killed in an automobile accident that involved drunk driving. You can well imagine the shock and horror of my whole family. This was definitely a bitter cup. Though all of us processed this news differently, we all knew that nothing would ever be the same again.

CONFUSED BELIEVERS

As we were in the midst of trying to deal with this, some well-intending Christians came to our home to "comfort" us. They told us that because of our sin, God had taken Jimmy. This brought anything but comfort. To me, it brought confusion and so many questions: "If I had gone, would God have killed me also?" "If our sins killed my brother (as a form of God's wrath), then how come our neighbors still have their kids? They were sinning as good or better than us."

To my mom, it brought guilt, anger, and resentment. She blamed herself and then God, carrying that bitterness the rest of her life which ended up taking her to an early grave. She processed this bitter cup in the wrong way. It wasn't until her death bed that she saw God for who He truly was, her loving heavenly Father who sent His Son to die for her and all her sins. On the other hand, I knew in my heart that God had not killed my brother, but the accident still left me numb and uncertain. I put my relationship with God on the back shelf and focused on tennis that much more. It wasn't until 1980 when I came back to God and gave Him my whole heart that I was able to fully process that bitter cup and become fruitful.

In this bitter cup, my mother experienced every possible symptom of Numbers 5. Hebrews 12:15 became a frightening reality in her life: *"looking carefully lest anyone fall short of the grace of God; lest any root of bitterness springing up cause trouble and by this many become defiled"* (NKJV). The lack of understanding of God's grace gave way to a misunderstanding of God's law and the curses revealed under Old Covenant law. This mishandling of law by well-meaning Christians, and a bitter cup that no mother should have to bear, caused her all kinds of trouble spiritually, mentally, and physically. The bitterness inside was her undoing.

On the other hand, because of an open vision in 1980, I was able to see the amazing grace of God in Jesus on the cross. I saw God gave His Son to save us from our sins—not taking our sons as a payment or penalty for our sins. To this day, I am thankful to know the love God has for me and my family. The grace message of God's love in my life overcame the law message of wrath. Praise God, my mother accepted Jesus as Lord on her death bed. While bitterness took her natural life, blessings are a part of her eternal life.

REJOICE—REALLY?!

The apostle James is a third witness of the importance of joy and good cheers during tribulations (bitter cups): *"My brethren, count it all joy when ye fall into divers temptations; Knowing this, that the trying of your faith worketh patience. But let patience have her perfect work, that ye may be perfect and entire, wanting nothing"* (James 1:2-4).

Count it all joy? Why do I have to count it all joy? Because no bitter cup ever feels good. Ever. How do I count it all joy? James says that we need to know something in a trial instead of wanting to feel something. What is it that we must know? We must know the character of our Husband. Our faith in Him is being tested. The trial doesn't mean we don't have faith but rather we do have faith, and it is being refined. If we are faithful in the trial, we can develop stronger faith, patience, and endurance. Being faithful to

Jesus (our Husband) brings about the maturity of character the Lord longs to see in us (His wife).

Years ago, a friend of mine overheard me complaining about my chest size and wishing it was bigger. He suggested I try some weights to increase it, so I purchased a small set of them. I watched those weights for more than a year, and there was no change. My friend lied! Those weights, in and of themselves, could not build my chest. I have to work out with the weights to experience the benefit. I have to resist and submit to the weights for thirty minutes a day, four days a week.

NO PAIN—NO GAIN

Trials, afflictions, and hardships do not mature us. Submitting to Jesus, being faithful to Him, and resisting the devil will bring about spiritual change in our lives. Standing on God's Word without doubt and regardless of my feelings or lack of understanding is what brings maturity. Maturity of character is not developed in or with problems alone; problems do not perfect us. Yet trusting our Husband, Jesus, and fighting the good fight of faith in our problems does build maturity of character. Faith and patience during trials bring about spiritual formation in our lives. Hebrews 6:12 says *"...be not slothful, but followers of them who through faith and patience inherit the promises."*

> Yet trusting our Husband, Jesus, and fighting the good fight of faith in our problems does build maturity of character.

One of those many promises is being conformed into the image of Jesus. When we combine faith and patience during the trials of this life, God brings good out of them and we are transformed. No one enjoys problems but be confident that God is at work in all areas and times of our lives. While He isn't causing us harm, He is working all things out for our good as we turn to Him in faith.

NEVER GIVE UP!

*That is why we never give up. Though our bodies are dying, our spirits are being renewed every day. For our **present troubles** are small and won't last very long. **Yet they produce for us a glory** that vastly outweighs them **and will last forever!** So we don't look at the troubles we can see now; rather, we fix our gaze on things that cannot be seen. For the things we see now will soon be gone, but the things we cannot see will last forever* (2 Corinthians 4:16-18 NLT).

The pressures of life, when countered with steadfast faith (faithfulness to Jesus), produce a strength for us that vastly outweighs the pressure. That is a blessing to know. As we remain faithful and steadfast in our love for Jesus, His glory is literally being worked from within us. As we look to Jesus in our focus, His glory is increasing in our lives. When Satan strikes us with problems, it ignites the passion of Jesus in our defense.

Remember the fireplace I built for Sue in our house? Remember how I nearly burned the house down because I didn't understand how presoaked logs worked? The more and the harder I struck those logs—thinking it would help put that fire out, the more the flames multiplied and grew. The intensity and ferocity of the fire was not abated, but it was furiously enhanced. When Satan foolishly strikes us with the trials and afflictions of life, it ignites the "glory" inside of us. Fire rises up in the heart of Jesus like a bright light, a roar of love for us, a good and pure and thorough defense. We can confidently know it, feel it, and hear His voice. He leads us through all things, encouraging us, and reassuring our hearts. His light overcomes fear and weakness.

> The pressures of life, when countered with steadfast faith (faithfulness to Jesus), produce a strength for us that vastly outweighs the pressure.

Then our enemies are the frightened ones.

LOOK OUT DEVIL!

When our Jesus is awakened for our defense, watch out devil! Our God is a consuming fire of passion toward us, with wrath against our enemies. There is a beautiful picture of this in a passage from Exodus 1 that embodies this concept: *"But the more the Egyptians oppressed them, the more the Israelites multiplied and spread, and the more alarmed the Egyptians became"* (Exodus 1:12 NLT).

Learn to draw near to the Lord in times of trouble. It is in our act of turning and trusting Him, totally dependent upon Him, that His passion for us is experienced and His vengeance toward our spiritual enemies is most assuredly executed. After all, *"...If God be for us, who can be against us?"* (Romans 8:31).

CHAPTER 12

SUBMISSION

*Wives, **submit** yourselves unto your own husbands,
as unto the Lord. For the husband is the head
of the wife, even as **Christ is the head of the
church**: and he is the savior of the body.*
—Ephesians 5:22-23

Few subjects evoke such intense negative emotions and flawed opinions as the word *submission*. The concept of submission to parents, teachers, police officers, civil authorities and, in some cases, even spiritual authorities can get almost everybody's dander up and the opinions flying. And here's the biggie: submission in marriage. *"Wives submit to your own husbands as unto the Lord."* ARE YOU KIDDING ME?! The mere mention of it can cause a meltdown or cardiac arrest (just kidding!). While I may be exaggerating to a measure, I have never brought the subject up at church without experiencing some pushback.

Wives should submit to their own husbands, but they are not required to submit to everyone's husbands. The kind of submission Ephesians 5 refers to is in the marriage relationship alone. My wife is required by God to submit to me as her husband, but she is not required to submit to all men within society at large, or even all men at church. I was actually taught that all women were to submit to all men. This is simply not true. With that said, let's look at submission

> Few subjects evoke such intense negative emotions and flawed opinions as the word *submission.*

between a husband and wife as God ordained it to be. Remember, we are really talking about the union between Christ and the Church. We are called to submit to Jesus as His bride.

SUBMISSION IN SCRIPTURE

Submission is very misunderstood, especially within the domestic realm of marriage. I believe this is by design of the enemy in order to distort the truth, power, and blessing of our submission to Jesus as a Husband. The husband is the head of the wife, even as Jesus is the head of the Church (see Ephesians 5:23). The headship of the earthly husband is not to be abusive, even as Jesus being our head is not abusive. In fact, Jesus is just the opposite. He treats His wife with excellent respect and unconditional love.

In every single case of an abuse of submission in marriage that I've encountered, the word itself is taken out of context of the whole of Scripture. A wife will find it easy to submit to a husband who loves unselfishly. As we see the blessing associated with submission in marriage, we can also see what a blessing it is to submit to Jesus. How the Bible defines submission in marriage should also apply wherever submission is mentioned in Scripture. For example, everyone is required to submit to all authority.

CIVIL AUTHORITIES

Everyone **must submit** *to governing authorities. For all authority comes from God, and those in positions of authority have been placed there by God. So anyone who rebels against authority is rebelling against what God has instituted, and they will be punished. For the authorities do not strike fear in people who are doing right, but in those who are doing wrong. Would you like to live without fear of the authorities? Do what is right, and they will honor you. The authorities are God's servants, sent for your good. But if you are doing wrong, of course you should be afraid, for they have the power to punish you. They are God's servants, sent for the very purpose of punishing those who do what is wrong. So* **you must submit to them***, not only to avoid punishment, but also to keep a clear conscience* (Romans 13:1-5 NLT).

Civil authority is ordained by God. We are commanded to submit to the powers that be. Civil authorities are called by God and accountable to God to punish evildoers and protect those who want to live in peace and harmony with our fellow man. That doesn't mean every civil worker is of God or godly, and that we are to obey and submit to an ungodly edict or law. If any government official directs me to do something that disobeys God, the Scriptures tell me I'm not required to obey. My obedience to man can never require disobedience to God.

EXAMPLES OF SUBMISSION

The apostles modeled this in Acts 4:17-18 and 5:28 when man commanded them *"not to speak in Jesus' name"* (NLT) after God told them to "go into all the world in My name" (see Matthew 28:19). God has called us all to do whatever we do in His name (see Colossians 3:17). There is no other name under heaven given whereby we must be saved (see Acts 4:12) When brought before a council (the authorities), to give an account for their disobedience to the command, Peter replied that they ought to obey God rather than man (see Acts 5:29). They were beaten and told again not speak in the name of Jesus. *"And they departed from the presence of the council, rejoicing that they were counted worthy to suffer shame for his name"* (Acts 5:41).

Once again, we have an example of Christian suffering (bitter cup), and they were of good cheer. That is awesome! It's important to note that the apostles didn't riot or rebel against authority. They did not leave the council and burn down the town. They didn't destroy local businesses or private property or rob their fellow man by looting. That would be committing unjust acts against the innocent in retaliation for an abuse of power. No, they suffered wrongfully and did it joyfully for Christ's sake—a concept few would even think about these days. When we do the right thing, and suffer wrongfully and take it patiently, that is acceptable to God. *"For what credit is it if, when you are beaten for your faults, you take it patiently, this is commendable before*

God. For to this you were called, because Christ also suffered for us, leaving us an example, that you should follow Hissteps" (1 Peter 2:20-21 NKJV).

Again, notice Peter's instructions to fellow believers. *"Yet if anyone suffers as a Christian, let him not be ashamed, but let him glorify God in this matter"* (1 Peter 4:16 NKJV).

Now let's look at what Peter wrote in his own epistle in regard to submitting to civil authorities. *"Submit yourselves to every ordinance of man for the Lord's sake: whether it be to the king, as supreme; or unto governors, as unto them that are sent by him for the punishment of evildoers, and for the praise of them that do well. For so is the will of God..."* (1 Peter 2:13-15).

Peter wrote we should submit to civil authorities, yet in Acts 5:29 he said to obey God over man. He remained submissive to authority in general but non-compliant to an ungodly order. While submission and obedience are closely related, they are not the same. It is possible to be submissive and not obedient or obedient and not submissive. An example of this would be when you tell your teenage son to take out the trash and he obeys but is murmuring and complaining the whole way. His actions reflected obedience, but his attitude was not submissive. Peter was punished wrongfully for doing the right thing and that was acceptable with God.

> While submission and obedience are closely related, they are not the same.

ABUSES VS. SUBMISSION

So, let's apply this to a husband and wife in marriage. Submission is an attitude of respect toward the office of husband; obedience is an action to a request or command of a husband. No wife is required by God to obey an ungodly command given by a husband, but she can remain submissive to the office. She should never violate God's Word or her conscience in regard to her husband's wishes, nor start a "hate all men" movement.

Notice Ananias and Sapphira in Acts 5:

> *But there was a certain man named Ananias who, with his wife, Sapphira, sold some property. He brought part of the money to the apostles, claiming it was the full amount. With his wife's consent, he kept the rest. Then Peter said, "Ananias, why have you let Satan fill your heart? You lied to the Holy Spirit, and you kept some of the money for yourself. The property was yours to sell or not sell, as you wished. And after selling it, the money was also yours to give away. How could you do a thing like this? You weren't lying to us but to God!" As soon as Ananias heard these words, he fell to the floor and died. Everyone who heard about it was terrified. Then some young men got up, wrapped him in a sheet, and took him out and buried him. About three hours later his wife came in, not knowing what had happened. Peter asked her, "Was this the price you and your husband received for your land?" "Yes," she replied, "that was the price." And Peter said, "How could the two of you even think of conspiring to test the Spirit of the*

Lord like this? The young men who buried your husband are just outside the door, and they will carry you out, too." Instantly, she fell to the floor and died. When the young men came in and saw that she was dead, they carried her out and buried her beside her husband (Acts 5:1-10 NLT).

In Acts 4:35-36, a man named Joseph sold some land and laid all of the proceeds at the apostles feet. Later a husband and wife team decided to claim to do the same thing. Ananias and Sapphira sold some property. Peter made it clear that the proceeds were theirs to do with as they wished. They did not have to bring the entire amount to the disciples and were free to take any amount anywhere they wanted or felt led by God. They could have kept it all, given some of it, or all of it. Any of that would have been pleasing to the Lord. Instead, their desire to be seen of men doing a noble act got the best of them. They gave the impression that they were giving all the money to the church.

REPENTANCE IS GOOD!

Ananias could have repented and avoided his severe judgment, but he stuck to his story and dropped dead at the apostle Peter's feet. Peter said he did not lie to man but to God. Hours later, Sapphira came into the service. Peter confronted her with questions regarding the sale of the property. She could have chosen not to go along with her husband's deception. Instead, she chose to submit to the lies, obey their plan, and stay the course her husband chose. She would have been better off to disobey and *not* submit to her husband. As soon as she lied, she dropped dead as well. When we follow errant leaders in the name of submission, we fall under the consequences of our error, just as Sapphira did.

Peter gave Ananias and Sapphira both ample room for repentance, but they both chose to lie to the Holy Spirit. Sapphira could have been respectful and submissive to her husband and the office of husband but refuse to obey him. In doing so, she would have obeyed God and not lied, and she should have obeyed God rather than man or her husband.

SUBMISSION AND DISAGREEMENT

Submission is required in matters of disagreement or opinion outside of conscience and moral law—biblical principles and God's definition of right and wrong. Submission isn't submission until we disagree. Let that sink in! Submission is the acknowledgment that someone is leading, and someone is following. Someone initiates and someone responds. Someone yields, and someone takes the pressure and responsibility as well as the accountability to lead, make the tough decisions and bear the consequences of those decisions, both good and bad.

> Submission isn't submission until we disagree. Let that sink in!

Submission is not cowering to the rulership of another. In its best form, it is yielding to the Holy Spirit. Sue submitting to me as her husband is healthy, and it's very easy if I love her as Christ loved the Church. Me submitting to Jesus is healthy, and Jesus submitting to the Father is as well. Yes, even Jesus submits. Christ sees us as joint heirs with Him. Husbands must see wives as co-laborers with equal value and worth. In a healthy marriage, wives have equality in loving submission to their husband as the leader, not the dictator or abuser.

Dictators rule for selfish gain. Leaders direct with the good of others in mind. Dictators demand with contradiction of character and lifestyle. Leaders guide by example of both. Dictators control and manipulate. Leaders coach and delegate.

I've heard submission likened to a captain and first mate on a ship. When a decision must be made, they will discuss the problem thoroughly and respectfully together in search of the best solution. Yet because a ship cannot go in two different directions at once, the captain is ultimately responsible and held accountable for the final decision good or bad. This is what God had in mind when He established the husband as head of the wife and the wife to submit to her husband. Sue and I submit one to another in the fear and the respect of the Lord. There is mutual love and honor. I am simply willing to bear the responsibility for our final decision in any given situation. All of this points back to Jesus as the head of us, the Church. How has Christ loved the Church? He is lovingly leading in all the affairs of this life. In grace He is abounding toward us with all good things. We simply need to submit as an act of faith and surrender.

SPIRITUAL AUTHORITIES

What about submission to spiritual authorities in the church?

*Remember your leaders who taught you the word of God. Think of all the good that has come from their lives, and follow the example of their faith. **Obey your*** *spiritual leaders, and do what they say. Their work is to watch over your souls, and they are accountable to God. Give them reason to do this with joy and not with sorrow. That would certainly not be for your benefit* (Hebrews 13:7,17 NLT).

Does obeying my spiritual leaders and doing what they say require me to obey an ungodly request of a pastor or other leaders in the church? Do I blindly follow leadership without question in order to be a submissive member of a church? Follow their example of faith, but never follow any example of sin or error.

Let me just say this quickly, if pastors treated men in church culture like some men treat their wives in marriage, the men would not submit! Whatever submission means in marriage, it also applies to pastor/parish relations.

While I don't believe we should "question" every decision our spiritual leaders make, we certainly should be free to ask questions concerning any direction the church takes. I'm under no obligation to support or follow a direction that violates clear scripture or my conscience. On the other hand, I'm not to protest the leadership's decisions out in the parking lot or create strife and division in the church.

As to civil government, I may not agree with everything going on today, but I'm not anti-government. I respect the authority of government, but I don't obey an ungodly request of any government. I respect spiritual authority as well. My submission in both cases is an attitude of reverence and respect; my obedience is an action in response to godliness or the Scriptures.

Abuse of authority is all too common in many segments of our society today. For many, the temptation is to throw the baby out with the dirty water and be done with all of it. Corruption in civil government is truly alarming but having no government and living under anarchy is worse. Corruption in church culture is very damaging and disheartening, but "...forsaking the assembling of ourselves..." is not an option (see Hebrews 10:25). The corruption and abuse of women in Hollywood is deplorable, but as of this writing, at least it is finally being exposed.

Sexual perversion in our culture always leads to the abuse of women and children. There is no place in any of these institutions for the mistreatment of women on any level. The marriage relationship is no exception. Our wives need to be loved and treated with honor and respect at all times. *"In the same way you married men should live considerately with [your wives], with an intelligent recognition [of the marriage relation], honoring the woman as [physically] the weaker, but [realizing that you] are joint heirs of the grace (God's unmerited favor) of life, in order that your prayers may not be hindered and cut off. [Otherwise you cannot pray effectively]"* (1 Peter 3:7 AMPC).

As His bride, Jesus treats us with honor and respect. We are the weaker vessel after the flesh, but He treats us as heirs together in the grace of life (joint heirs with Him). We need an intelligent biblical understanding of our union with Christ. We need our minds renewed to view Him as a tremendous blessing to us. He is nothing like corrupt civil authorities, abusive husbands, or overbearing and controlling pastors or leaders. Our prayers become effectual when we dwell with Jesus according to the new creation. Never fear submitting to Jesus.

SABBATH REST

The beauty and Sabbath rest of the Christian life is learning to submit. Learn to agree with Him when your carnal, unrenewed mind wants to disagree. Learn to yield to His will rather than your own opinions and desires. Respect and honor God's Word above your feelings, philosophy, or opinions or the opinions and philosophies of others, especially most of the media and Hollywood. When the world claims one thing and my Husband claims another, I submit to the leadership of my Husband. Jesus will never lead me astray. I'm married to Him and not the "popular opinion" of this world. I've learned over the years to divorce myself from philosophies, vain deceit, and the traditions of men and submit to the thoughts and ways of my Husband. Many submit to and obey things in our culture that demand they disobey Jesus and His Word.

JESUS AND SUBMISSION

In turn, Jesus submits to us in the sense that He never imposes or manipulates us in regard to His will. He never condemns until we comply with His desires. And even if He knows it is for our own good, He will not push or shove us. He never overrides our will or forces His love on us. This is why seeking Him and learning to yield and submit is so important. While He has provided every good thing we need in grace, it must be reccived by faith (Ephesians 2:8).

> As His bride, Jesus treats us with honor and respect.

In the marriage relation, Sue and I submit one to another. Before Paul speaks of the submission of a wife to her own husband in Ephesians 5:22, look at verse 21. *"And further, submit to one another out of reverence for Christ"* (NLT).

We are to be filled with the Spirit, submitting one to another in a healthy relationship. While there is a greater responsibility on the wife to submit, we as co-laborers together of the grace of life submit to each other in most issues of our lives together as "one flesh."

Jesus has modeled submission in His relationship with the heavenly Father:

- He didn't do anything unless He saw the Father do it first (John 5:19).

- He didn't say anything until He heard the Father say it (John 5:30).

- He was water baptized by John in submission (Matthew 3:13-17).

- His complete submission to the Father lead to the ultimate act of obedience—the death of the cross (Philippians 2:8).

- He constantly prayed before He acted (a sign of submission) (Matthew 26:36).

- He prayed "not my will but Thine be done" (John 5:30, Matthew 26:39).

- He was submissive and obedient to Mary and Joseph (Luke 2:50-52). This was after He knew God was His actual Father.

In Genesis 2, we see God and man working together, submitting one to another. God was bringing all the animals to Adam, but Adam was naming them. When Adam named an animal, that was the name. Period. God didn't override him or overrule him. God had the power and brought the animals, but Adam had the authority and named them. It was God and man working together—grace and faith in a marriage relation. God was leading, but not in an oppressive, domineering way. God actually submitted to Adam in the naming of all the animals. WOW! How cool is that! Consider Matthew 18:18: *"Verily I say unto you, Whatsoever ye shall bind on earth shall be bound in heaven: and whatsoever ye shall loose on earth shall be loosed in heaven."*

Notice whatsoever *we—not God*—bind on earth will be bound in heaven, and whatsoever *we—not God*—loose on earth will be loosed in heaven. If two of us agree on earth, it will be done of the Father in heaven. Once again, God and man are co-laborers together on the earth submitting one to another. So many blame God for all the things wrong in their lives, not realizing they are submitting to something beside God. Don't submit to sin; submit to Jesus and overcome sin. Don't submit to sickness. Submit to Jesus and by His stripes you are healed. Don't submit to poverty. Submit to Jesus who wishes above all things that you prosper and be in health (see 3 John 2). Submit unto God and resist the devil, and he will flee (see James 4:7). We don't have to submit to fear, worry, or anxiety, but we can fully submit to Jesus in all of life's challenges, knowing He is our faithful Husband.

CHURCH FIRE

Submitting to the Lord in the good and the bad times is a key to victory. In June of 2002, I was working from home when I got a call from my son Jacob, "Dad, are you sitting down?"

Oh no! I thought, *this can't be good.* Being stubborn, I kept standing and asked, "What's going on?"

"The church is on fire!" Jacob replied.

At that moment I sincerely wished I had submitted to my son and sat down. After sitting down, I asked, "What do you mean the church is on fire?"

"You just need to come to the church, Dad, and right now!" he said.

Even though my heart was sinking like a rock in a pond, he gave me some peace by letting me know that everyone had gotten out in time and, so far, nobody had been hurt. I grabbed my keys and headed out the door.

We live fifteen miles from the church, and let me tell you, that was the longest twenty-minute drive of my life, especially since I could already see smoke from that direction. This was no small fire, and the smoke kept getting worse the closer I got. I cannot begin to describe the vast array of emotions going on inside of me. Getting control of those emotions was not going to be easy, but I knew I had to do it. Praying in English and praying in the Spirit were the only ways I could keep my thoughts from running wild. I knew I had to keep my mind focused on getting to the church safely and without a speeding ticket.

As I pulled into the parking lot, the scene before me was something right out of a nightmare. Our chapel building, where we held children's church and the youth service, normally sat next to our main sanctuary building. We were scheduled to begin a youth camp that very evening, but the chapel didn't sit there anymore. Now, it was just a smoldering pile of rubble, and the fire was raging through our main sanctuary building. There was nothing I could do.

> As I pulled into the parking lot, the scene before me was something right out of a nightmare.

I stood there praying and watched as firefighters worked feverishly to get it all under control. I could hear people talking and crying all around me as the memories of our humble beginnings were going through their minds—weddings, salvations, and many altar experiences with God. All that went up in a dark, black smoke cloud that filled the Durant, Oklahoma skies.

LORD—YOU HAVE A PROBLEM

By the time they put it out, the chapel building was completely gone, and there was a gaping hole in our main sanctuary that looked like a semi-truck straight out of the devil's hell had smashed through it. There was well over two million dollars in damage, and Sunday was coming. Many people there were mourning their beloved gathering place. It held so many memories for each of them, as it did for me. I knew I was expected to lead us all through this tragedy. I also knew I couldn't do it by myself. At that point, there was nothing in the natural I could do to fix this, and I felt pretty alone and dazed.

With strong resolve and in a determined way, I thought, *You have to cast your care on the Lord.* The best way I knew to do that was to have a conversation with Him while I was standing in that parking lot, looking at years of hard work and an immense labor of love that, in a matter of a few hours, had all gone up in a puff of smoke. I paused, looked up sincerely, and then prayed, "Lord, You have a problem. This is Your church, these are Your people, so this is Your problem. I promise that I will not leave or forsake You. I will stay with You to the very end." This was my way of submitting to the Lord, my Husband, and trusting Him with all my heart, determined to lean not on my own understanding (see Proverbs 3:5).

GOD'S PERSPECTIVE

As a pastor, I had heard too many people view things as "their problem" and God was forsaking them. So I just reversed it in my conversation with the Lord. Even though this was probably the hardest thing we had been through up to that point, I saw God work miracles in the hearts and lives of our precious congregation. We pulled together to rebuild, and in the process, we saw God's grace in new dimensions. One miracle was that the rest of that year boasted the greatest growth we had seen in a six-month period.

Time would fail me if I were to share all the wonderful things God did in our midst. The key to the success of this story, however, is that together we chose to submit to Jesus and follow Him closely as He led us through the difficulties (a bitter cup). We drew near to God in that season of difficulty and He certainly drew nigh to us. Submission to Jesus is something we should never fear as

His beloved wife. He is a worthy and faithful Husband in all our circumstances. In your submission to Him, know that He wills nothing but good for you.

CHAPTER 13

BEHOLDING THE GLORY

To whom God would make known what is the riches
*of the **glory** of this mystery among the Gentiles*
*which is Christ in you, the **hope of glory**.*
—Colossians 1:27

Just like a wedding doesn't make a marriage, a new convert doesn't make a disciple. The wedding is the first step toward a life of adventure in the building of a marriage. Getting saved and becoming a convert is the first step toward the adventure of being a disciple. The difference between a convert and a disciple is simple: converts are immature while a disciple is maturing in his or her relationship with the Lord. When we get saved, we are an immature bride to Jesus, however, we can grow and mature in that union and marriage. I hope I'm not the only one who has changed since I married my wife. I know I'm not the only one who has changed since receiving Christ (got married).

There are things that can enhance or hinder the maturing process between a husband and wife, and it is the same in our relationship with Jesus. We start out in an immature way, and figure it out as we go along. Over the years of my own maturing, I've discovered some "rhythms of grace," or proven disciplines tested over centuries and found sound. These disciplines can take us from converts to strong disciples. They are habits for daily life that have a *beat* to them as they are exercised regularly throughout the day. These are simple regimens such as attentively reading the Bible, speaking the Word out loud, continual prayer, and learning to become still in order to hear our Husband speak to us. That "still small voice" is crucial to our Christian walk. Actually, Jesus is so very close to us that when He speaks, it's more like a whisper.

> Just like a wedding doesn't make a marriage, a new convert doesn't make a disciple.

RHYTHMS OF GRACE

As a good wife, one of the many rhythms of grace that needs to be developed is *focus*. Developing focus is such a powerful principle in our lives. Your dominant thoughts and focus are what control your life. Proverbs 23:7 says it best, *"For as he thinketh in his heart, so is he....."* Jesus said it this way, *"The light of the body is the eye: if therefor thine eye be single, thy whole body shall be full of light"* (Matthew 6:22).

Notice again, what we focus on, will fill us. A single eye is one focused on Jesus and His Word. It's easy to focus on the wrong things. People can let themselves become captives of everything in this world. They stare at the circumstances around them and only *glance* at God. They constantly look at their problems, and as a result, worry becomes man's underlying meditation. Worry is actually meditation on a type of death. Death is part of all things associated with darkness and negativity, such as: "The glass is half *empty* not half full." "God never blesses me" or "I'll never get that promotion."

The truth is, God has called us to the very opposite of death and darkness. He calls us to behold His love and provision, which He longs to manifest. He says, "Keep your eyes on ME, and only glance at the things of the fallen world." Jesus challenged us to have faith in God who cares deeply about us. *"And why take ye thought for raiment? Consider the lilies of the field, how they grow; they toil not, neither do they spin: And yet I say unto you, that even Solomon in all his glory was not arrayed like one of these. Wherefore, if God so clothe the grass of the field, which today is, and to morrow is cast into the oven, shall he not much more clothe you, O ye of little faith?"* (Matthew 6:28-30).

BROKEN FOCUS

We need to behold the lilies of the field to behold their beauty and the magnificence of God's workmanship. They don't work or make their own clothes or wear jewelry, yet they are so gorgeous. Solomon was beautifully adorned with fine clothing, but not even Solomon was as beautiful as the lilies kissed by the morning dew. If He provides for the lilies, why are you losing sleep? Why are you upset? Have faith in your Husband's provision and protection of you! Don't you know who you are? Don't you know you are married to Jesus and that you married into wealth and provisions? If you are filled with anxiety, worry, and fret, then you can be sure you have problems that are self-induced and caused by a lack of beholding the right thing. We need to behold Jesus as our answer to any and all our problems. We need to always behold His great love for us. And we need to allow ourselves to *be held* by His love, so that as we go about our day, we will see everything through the prism of God's eyes.

In Second Corinthians 3, Paul compared Old Testament administration with the New Testament. The old brought condemnation and death while the new brought the life and bright light of righteousness and grace. Moses beheld the glory of the Lord when he received the Ten Commandments on Mount Sinai. When he came down from the mountain, the glory of God was like the sun, shining so brightly on him that the people couldn't look at it. He had to cover his face with a veil until it faded.

FREEDOM

The law would soon be superseded by the grace of God shown through Jesus Christ. So, Paul was in awe of the exceedingly great glory of God, and he exclaimed, *"...If that which was but passing and fading away came with such splendor, how much more must that which remains and is permanent abide in glory and splendor!"* (2 Corinthians 3:11 AMPC). Then, in verse 17, Paul rejoiced even more about the greatness of God that was spoken of concerning us—the people of God. *"Now the Lord is that Spirit: and where the Spirit of the Lord is, there is liberty"* (2 Corinthians 3:17).

Liberty refers to emancipation from bondage. In America, we celebrate our liberty every July Fourth. We celebrate our freedom from tyranny, our freedom to worship God, our freedom to speak the truth in love, and our freedom to exercise our faith without fear of persecution, prosecution, or execution from the government we empower. We celebrate that holiday once a year. As New Testament believers, we are to be celebrating our liberty in Christ every day of our lives because God has made us truly and eternally free. This is not about being free *to* sin as some people have asserted. The liberty that Jesus has brought us is freedom *from* sin.

It is the freedom to walk in the strength and wisdom of God and to grow in relationship with Him. We are now free to love Him, to love people, and to fulfill our destinies. We are free in Christ to be the workmanship that God created us to be before the foundation of the world (see Ephesians 2:10). We are free to be blessed and a blessing everywhere we go. We're free from sin's tyranny! Sin's dominion is broken over us by God's amazing grace displayed in

> "Sin's dominion is broken over us by God's amazing grace displayed in the fact He would marry us."

the fact He would marry us (see Romans 6:14). After all, we were not the cream of the crop; or, at least, I wasn't. Christ in me, Duane, is surely the hope and great mystery of glory!

FREE FROM WRATH

Paul tells us in Second Corinthians 3:17 that when the Spirit of the Lord is in our hearts, we are free to serve and walk with God. We are free from God's wrath and the curses of the law (Galatians 3:13). We are free from the condemnation that holds so many people back from doing great things (Romans 8:1). In our new condition in Christ, we are privileged to run to God when we fail or sin. Being secure in our union with Jesus, we can work things out when we mess up. We are not wed to our mistakes any longer because we are wed to Jesus and His very righteousness that no sin can put asunder.

BEHOLD THE GLORY

*But we all, with open face **beholding** as in a glass the **glory** of the Lord, are changed into the same image from **glory to glory**, even as by the Spirit of the Lord* (2 Corinthians 3:18).

Within this passage is the power and process of change. It can have a profound impact on the recovery of our true identity and can give all of us the ever-increasing ability to comprehend the tender and magnificent way God has embraced us.

Instinctively, in the deepest parts of our hearts, we all know that we are hardwired by God for change. The Scriptures declare that God's will for us involves continually being conformed into the image of His dear Son (see Romans 8:29). However, many fear change. That is primarily because, in the past, they determined to change and even began to change until something tripped them up, and they found themselves back at the starting gate. "Back to square one" usually isn't too bad when it happens once or twice, but to have started up the mountain of change only to get knocked down to the bottom of it time and time again can be very discouraging. Proverbs 13:12 sums my thought up nicely, *"Hope deferred makes the heart "* (NKJV). Getting our hopes up for change and being disappointed can take a toll on us.

So, why do we as believers, created in Christ, fail so often at change? I believe there are several reasons. The fear of negative judgments and false accusations concerning our sincere desire to change can be very disheartening. Statements like "She is such a hypocrite" or "He never really intended to change" or "It's just empty talk, he never really does it" are very real weapons Satan uses against us to cancel out positive change and lock us into the destructive cycles of our pasts.

But what if change were easier than we thought? What if it could happen independent of our human abilities or even the lack thereof? What if we could see progressive success instead of chronic failure? Remember the Proverbs scripture we talked about earlier? Well, there's more to it: *"Hope deferred maketh the heart sick: but when the desire cometh, it is a tree of life"* (Proverbs 13:12).

When the desired change comes, it is a tree of life—a place of refuge and stability. Experiencing a permanent change is such a blessing and a joy to us as believers. But, none of us can change without the empowerment of God through the Holy Spirit that comes from within. We've all tried changing outside of that and failed miserably. That's why we've got to stop trying and start trusting.

When you first get saved, you keep trying to change this and that by sheer determination and willpower. You fail and you fail until one day you wake up and say, "I can't do this. I can't live trying to change." To which God says, "Good! That's exactly where I want you. That's where I *need* you. You *can't* try to change. Let Me live the change in you and through you." It is at this point that you enter what I call the rhythms of grace for your life and begin to allow the Living Word to lead you into the recovery of your true identity. When we transition from trying in our human ability and willpower to trusting in God's grace through faith, change by God's Spirit simply occurs. I know for many that sounds too good to be true, but it really is a fact.

Before we look at the entire process of change revealed in Second Corinthians 3:18, we must understand that everything hinges on beholding the glory. We cannot see or experience change beholding our sin. Change only comes from beholding God's glory, which is our new condition united to Christ. I'm not saying we ignore or deny any sin in our lives but dwelling on or in them will not change anything. If change comes from beholding God's glory, then we must understand His glory, and God's glory is exactly what Jesus came to reveal. Consider the apostle John's writing: "*So the Word became human and made his home among us. He was full of unfailing love and faithfulness. And we have seen his glory, the glory of the Father's one and only Son*" (John 1:14 NLT).

> When we transition from trying in our human ability and willpower to trusting in God's grace through faith, change by God's Spirit simply occurs.

If we see Jesus, we have seen God's glory and His unfailing love and faithfulness to us. Seeing Him as our Husband and seeing His great love for us, His bride, is a part of His glory. Seeing Him united to us and forever with us involved His glory, "*Christ in you* [us], *the hope of glory*" (Colossians 1:27). "*The Son radiates God's own glory and expresses the very character of God...*" (Hebrews 1:3 NLT).

The glory of God is His personhood. It is His character and true nature of a loving and faithful Husband. The goodness of God is His glory and that's what leads us to repentance or lasting change (see Romans 2:4). His glory involves His kindness and mercy. In Exodus 33, Moses asks to see the glory of God, and God said He will make His goodness pass by and proclaim His name. He spoke of His graciousness and compassion. He then mentions not being able to see His face and survive in our human condition or bodies. The face of God is His personhood and fullness of His being (glory). He put Moses in the cleft of a rock and covered Him with His hand. He passed and declared His back to Moses. Exodus 34:6-7 is where He declares His back side versus His face: *"And the Lord passed before him and proclaimed, 'The LORD, the LORD God, merciful and gracious, longsuffering, and abounding in goodness and truth, keeping mercy for thousands, forgiving iniquity and transgression and sin, by no means clearing the guilty, visiting the iniquity of the fathers upon the children and the children's children to the third and the fourth generation'"* (NKJV).

Simply put, the glory of God is His goodness and kindness. As we behold His love for us and mercy toward us, we are changed. It's not God's wrath and anger, but His mercy that brings lasting change. The great mystery of God's love for us revealed in Jesus as the faithful Husband to us, His bride, produces supernatural change. By beholding Jesus (God's glory) and His complete work of the cross, change becomes certain and lasting. The change of our old identity in Adam to our new identity in Christ is a part of beholding His glory. Everything we do comes out of who we believe we are. You're His bride, not a widow. You're wed to the Messiah of the world; that's great glory!

OUR NEW NAME

We have a new name. When a woman marries a man, she has a name change signifying a new condition in union with her husband. Sue became Mrs. Duane Sheriff. When we get saved or born again, we get a new name, *Christian*. That name was given to us by unbelievers because they saw Christ in us (Acts 11:26). Throughout Scripture God changed people's names when they went from unbelief to faith in God. Saul the persecutor became Paul the preacher. Through his new identity in Christ, the Lord's bride, he went on to write nearly two-thirds of the New Testament. Rahab the Harlot had her name changed when by faith she hid the spies from danger before the Jericho walls came down. We know she had a changed life by marrying an Israelite, Salmon, after God saved her and her family when Jericho was invaded by the Hebrews. Through marriage she brought forth the godly lineage that brought Jesus to the earth. She went from Rahab the Harlot to Rahab the great-great grandmother of David, the king. How's that for the impact of beholding the glory (Matthew 1:5-6)? Her lineage through David ushered in the Messiah of the world!

Jacob was a manipulator and deceiver, who wrestled with God. When he finally submitted, God changed his name. He went from Jacob "heel-catcher (supplanter)" to Israel "prince of God," "one conquered by God" (see Genesis 32:22-32). God is known as the God of Abraham, Isaac, and Jacob. Esau was the older brother of Jacob, and Jewish tradition dictated that as the oldest, Esau, was to receive the father's blessing. Yet he sold that right for a bowl of soup. God would have been known as the God of Abraham, Isaac, and Esau. What kind of glory did it take in Jacob's life to forever alter how God is known? That is so awesome! Abraham had his name changed from Abram "exalted father" to Abraham "father of many nations." His faith brought about a new identity that has affected the whole world. Glory to God!

What names were you called before Christ? What name do you have after Christ? Which one are you going to behold releasing supernatural change? Bride of Christ covers it all for me. Poor was my middle name and label that many imposed on me, and I ended up self- imposing as well. When I married Jesus, I married into wealth. I inherited God, His Kingdom, and every blessing heaven itself contained. I hit the

> When I married Jesus, I married into wealth. I inherited God, His Kingdom, and every blessing heaven itself contained.

mother lode. Gold digger envy has hit my whole family! We've been named heirs of God, more than conquerors, world overcomers, and more. Whether you know it or not, a name change *has* happened in your own marriage to Jesus that is glorious and powerful. Behold it in Jesus and change is coming to you and this world. The change has already happened in your spirit. Learn to behold it.

HOW TO CHANGE

*But we all, with open face beholding as in a glass the glory of the Lord, **are changed** into the same image from glory to glory, **even as by the Spirit of the Lord*** (2 Corinthians 3:18).

God has provided a means by which effortless, progressive, supernatural change can transpire in every believer's life...for a lifetime. Notice that change comes from "beholding in a glass" the glory of God. *Glass* here simply means *mirror*. This is referring to God's Word that is a mirror of the spirit world or God's Kingdom. God's Word reveals the condition of my spirit man that is united to Jesus, the hope of glory. God's Word is vital to real change. When the Scriptures declare you to be righteous and holy, that's speaking of your spirit, not your flesh. As we behold the glory of God in our spirit man, we are changed.

The Greek word for change is *metamorphoo*, and it is the root of our English word "metamorphosis." We've all learned in school that metamorphosis is the radical transformation of the structure of an animal by supernatural means. It's a caterpillar turning into a butterfly or a tadpole becoming a bullfrog. This doesn't happen in the blink of an eye—it's a process. A metamorphosis comes from the inside out. The Church often teaches that the caterpillar and the butterfly are a type of the new birth.

Yet God didn't use *metamorphoo* as a type of the new birth; He used it to illustrate the changes that occur in the believer's life through renewing our minds. Notice Romans 12:1-2 (NKJV) and the power of having our minds renewed:

> *I beseech you therefore, brethren, by the mercies of God that you present your bodies a living sacrifice, holy, acceptable unto God, which is your reasonable service. And do not conformed to this world, but be **transformed** by the renewing of your mind, that you might*

prove what is that good and acceptable and perfect will of God.

The New Living Translation of verse two reads: *"...but let God transform you into a new person by changing the way you think...."* We have to change the way we think since we entered into a marriage relationship with Jesus.

God is the one who changes our thinking as we set our mind on Him and choose to give Him our thoughts. This concept is actually new to most of us and is huge in the process of change. God changes our mind as we yield it to Him. The word "transformed" in this verse is also a translation of *metamorphoo.* Again, God used it in connection with mind renewal—not the new birth. You don't think your way into getting saved. You get saved by calling upon the name of the Lord. When you do, God rips out the stony heart and puts in a new, soft heart of flesh; He unites your spirit with His Spirit. He makes a new covenant with you, and He abides on the inside of you in the person of the Lord Jesus Christ.

In my book *Identity Theft,* I deal with the heart and how we are three parts: spirit, soul, and body. The renewing of our mind is vital to our success in the Christian life because the soul and how we think affects the spirit or the body. That book is worth getting even for just the chapters on spirit, soul, and body. God made and created us to be dominated by our spirit, but that won't happen independent of the soul (our mind, will, and emotions). We must yield our thoughts, emotions, opinions, and belief systems to God for Him to change them, thereby, changing our attitudes and actions.

Some critics think that Christians are just "mindless drones," but this supernatural change comes from the "renewing" of your mind, not the "removing" of it. We are not changed by being mere "followers" without thinking at all. Rather, we are changed by taking responsibility for the thoughts we choose to think on. Religion and the world try to conform us and change us from without, but God changes us by His Spirit from within. True Christianity is not religion; it is a relationship with the living God in the person of Jesus by the agency of the Holy Spirit in accordance with the Word of God. True mind renewal comes from within us as we choose to give God the tablets of our hearts. From our spirits, God renews our minds as we yield our thoughts to Him.

> Religion and the world try to conform us and change us from without, but God changes us by His Spirit from within.

This change in our lives is totally radical, just like a caterpillar turning into a butterfly. That's not instant, it takes discipline. The caterpillar has to dodge and avoid the birds. It has to struggle and climb up a tree and find a limb. It has to spin a cocoon. It has to work in the cocoon and then struggle its way out and then— BOOM! It explodes into a beautiful butterfly. That process takes time. If, in the name of love and compassion, we try to help him open the cocoon, we'd kill the butterfly. It has to struggle. It has to strain and relax and strain and relax. Many people want others to help bust them out of their cocoons, but they need to break out by their own cooperation with the Spirit and the

Word of God. If we could change on our own, we would receive the glory. If others could change us, they would receive the glory. But if change comes from the Spirit of God, then only He receives all the praise.

When I say effortless change, I'm not saying we have no part to play in the process. We choose what we think on, but God is the One who empowers those choices to bring about change. The struggle and battle are to stay focused, keeping your mind stayed or fixed on the Lord. Most of the spiritual warfare in the Christian life is in our thoughts, beliefs, emotions, and imagery that is a part of our soul. When we believe the lies of this world or false teachings about God, it is a battle to realign those thoughts. Prayer, praise and worship, and Bible reading are ways of keeping our minds stayed on the Lord and yielding our thoughts to God for positive change to occur. This is how we learn to not be moved by what we see and feel, but only by God's Word. His Word is truth! In time and by the Spirit, truth as we come to know it, sets us free (see John 8:32)—free from our old way of thinking and now free for supernatural change to occur.

It's a beautiful life when you know where the change comes from. The caterpillar has everything on the inside to enable him to fly; he just has to go through a metamorphose. The tadpole has everything on the inside that enables him to jump and croak like a bullfrog; he just needs to go through a process of radical change. We have everything inside our spirit through our marriage to Jesus to overcome anything in this life; we just need to be transformed by the renewing of our minds as we continually behold the glory of God in the finished work of Christ.

GLORY TO GLORY

"But we all with open face beholding as in a glass the Glory of the Lord, are changed into the same image from glory to glory." Our change is primarily progressive from glory to another measure of glory. I have experienced this in my own walk with Christ. I believe things can change quickly, but that is more the exception than the rule. I've seen people delivered from drugs instantly with no withdrawals—even the drugs that are so addictive that it would normally take a detox center to safely come off them. I've seen many people delivered from cigarettes and the addictive power of nicotine, and they never smoked again. I've seen alcoholics set free from alcoholism, and the list goes on. Yet while I do know that miracles in regard to change exist, I have found that my primary experience is that we go from glory to glory, faith to faith, grace and then more grace. That's not a bad thing either. It's a God thing!

In some cases, the process can be more beneficial than the deliverance itself or the change. We can learn things about ourselves (self-awareness) that God wants to change and more about how to interact positively with others. The process can be a very reflective and productive time in our relationship with the Lord. For me personally, I have noticed that the process has birthed ten times more patience in me than the way I was twenty years ago. Most importantly, going through the process has deepened my love for God and for people. The fellowship we have with Jesus and knowing Him in that fellowship is as beneficial as the power of His resurrection that produces change. The "glory to glory" victory we mentioned earlier becomes a series of steps that gets better and better results. That's good news to me, and that should be good news for you too! Don't be frustrated by the process of change in yourself or others; embrace it.

CHANGED BY GOD

"But we all with open face beholding as in a glass the Glory of the Lord, are changed into the same image from glory to glory, even by the Spirit of the Lord." Notice that change comes by the Spirit of the Lord. It doesn't come from self-effort, willpower, or trying a little harder. I can't change myself, much less my wife, children, or brothers and sisters in the Lord. God changes us supernaturally as we focus on His glory that is in Christ Jesus in each of us. Beholding the glory of God in me facilitates supernatural change. Beholding the good in me and

> God changes us supernaturally as we focus on His glory that is in Christ Jesus in each of us.

acknowledging all of Christ's goodness in me causes faith to become an effectual work in my life. *"That the communication of thy faith may become effectual by the acknowledging of every good thing which is in you in Christ Jesus"* (Philemon 1:6).

When we learn to see and acknowledge Christ's goodness in others, they also will experience positive, progressive, lasting change. I'm going to see more of Jesus in my natural life, beholding the real me in Christ in the mirror of His Word. This is the continual work of God's amazing grace. I'm not struggling to change because I am not using human ability or human wisdom. There is no glory in self-effort, but there is tremendous glory in the cross. The Spirit is taking me from being a convert (immature) to being a disciple (mature) in Christ. Thank You, Jesus, for marrying me and joining yourself to my spirit and now helping me work and walk it out in my daily life!

CHAPTER 14

MEDITATION

Since you have been raised to new life with Christ, **set
your sight** *on the realities of heaven, where Christ sits
in the place of honor at God's right hand.* **Think about**
*the things of heaven, not the things of earth. For you died
to this life, and* **your real life is hidden with Christ
in God.** *And when Christ, who is your life, is revealed
to the whole world, you will share in all his glory.*
—Colossians 3:1-4 NLT

These verses are dealing with the way we think. Having a healthy
thought life is so important because our thoughts affect what we
see, how we hear, and what we do. Many Christians live their
entire lives in defeat when they've got the life of Christ dwelling mightily within them, ready and waiting to operate through
them. They end up living their whole life in the caterpillar or tadpole stage because they neglect to think on heavenly realities and
go through the metamorphosis that comes from the renewing of
our minds.

One of the primary ways our minds are renewed is through Christian meditation. Meditation is a crucial spiritual discipline, one of those "rhythms of grace" I mentioned in an earlier chapter. Meditation is how we behold the glory. To meditate is to ponder or to think deeply on something. In the Hebrew and Greek, the word literally means "to mutter." Some think they are meditating because they memorize Scripture. But while memorizing Scripture is a good thing to do, mind renewal does not come from it. It comes from actually meditating on God in His Word. Meditation is more than a mental exercise. It is a form of prayer that creates the opportunity for God to bring light into the darkness and break the strongholds in your mind.

> **Meditation is how we behold the glory.**

When we meditate on God through His Word, we are giving ourselves over to a passage or governing principle of God's Kingdom. When we meditate on His love for us, we are giving ourselves over to the support, loyalty, and mightiness of that love. He desires that we set our sights on all the things of heaven and meditate on those heavenly realities instead of earthly distractions. We must continually seek God's perspective in all things because in doing so we declare Christ to be our life's source. Meditation helps us discover His attributes within us and remind us that we no longer belong to ourselves or the world. We are to leave the ways and thoughts of this world and cleave to Jesus and the mind of Christ (Isaiah 55:7).

We were all created to meditate. In fact, we meditate day and night on something; we just don't always know it. Either we are meditating on God, His goodness, and His love for us or the problems and challenges of this life. Meditating on God's love creates and causes faith to work (see Galatians 5:6). Meditating on the negative things of this life creates and causes fear and doubt to dominate us. It is our choice what we meditate on—not whether or not we meditate. When I've shared in the past on meditation, I've received pushback from many Christians. They say things like: "That sounds like some Middle Eastern religion." "Are you talking about transcendental meditation?" Some even mock saying, "You're just telling us to sit around and hum all day." Others ask, "Are you talking about mind over matter or Christian Science?"

Let me start by pointing out that all the prophets of the old covenant and the apostles of the new covenant were from the Middle East. The Bible came out of the Middle East. Next, I'm not talking about transcendental meditation or crystals or sitting around with our legs crossed, chanting, "Ohm.... Ohm...." I'm talking about a serious biblical, Christian discipline that invites God to renovate your thought processes. From a biblical perspective, meditation is not "mind over matter" but rather the truth of how your "mind matters" in regard to faith in God.

When we choose to meditate on the natural circumstances we all face daily, we are dominated by negative thoughts, then feelings, and eventually our actions. *No one loves or cares for me. Things never go my way. I'll never get ahead.* When we choose to meditate on God's Word and our new identity in Christ (His bride), our thoughts are renewed, feelings change, and then actions simply follow. *God loves me and I am blessed. God works everything together for my good. I'm blessed and highly favored by God and man. I'm the head and not the tail because of Jesus.* When we choose to think on

God and see life from His perspective, then our lives get renewed as well as our minds.

Meditation is the primary way we *set* our minds on the things above (see Colossians 3:1). As we set our minds on God and His goodness, the Holy Spirit is able to displace our negative, destructive thoughts and replace them with God's thoughts of life and peace. Meditation is not a "religious exercise" but rather a "relational discipline" with God. As we meditate on His words to us, we allow the Holy Spirit to begin to tear down walls, evicting all thoughts that will lead to death. As we meditate on Him, the Holy Spirit brings the life of Christ into our minds, transforming our lives.

THE POWER OF IMAGINATION

Another part of meditation is imagination. A lot of people think that imagination in and of itself is evil, but it is God who gave you your imagination. He gave you the ability to see things the way they could or should be even when they aren't at the moment. In fact, you are not really meditating on the things of God until you can visualize them in your imagination. That's good news!

> Meditation is not a "religious exercise" but rather a "relational discipline" with God.

Thank the Lord you can take His infallible Word and create new images of who you are and how your world should work. When you meditate on His promises to you, it allows Him to give you new images of prosperity and a successful outcome despite your current circumstances.

Years ago, I began to meditate on the Word of God and His will to prosper me in order to change the image of poverty on the inside into one of abundance and success. My vision of poverty was a part of my imagery that had to be renewed. Because of deep poverty in my family during my upbringing, I needed a vision (image) of prosperity in my heart.

A vision involves our hopes, desires, and dreams. *"Where there is no vision the people perish..."* (Proverbs 29:18). God is saying that when we don't have a clear vision of His will for us, we perish. Meditation opens the door of our hearts for godly hopes and desires to be enlarged and fueled in our hearts.

GOD'S GOOD WILL

John makes a profound statement in regard to God's will for our lives, *"Beloved, I wish above all things that thou mayest prosper and be in health, even as thy soul prospereth"* (3 John 2). This verse clearly shows that prosperity and health are connected to the condition of your soul (thought life). Your life will go the way of your dominate thoughts and images. Because images of poverty, lack, and low self-esteem dominated my mind for much of my life, it took a while to see myself as prosperous in finances and other areas of life.

Today, I would have to work hard to see myself as anything but blessed and highly favored of the Lord. My life was transformed by the renewing of my mind, which included meditation—picturing myself prosperous and seeing myself healthy. That process continues daily. God told Joshua how to prosper in his new assignment. Following the ministry of Moses and accomplishing what Moses did not (Israel into the Promised Land), was no small assignment. Joshua, like you or me, needed to be encouraged.

There shall not any man be able to stand before thee all the days of your life: as I was with Moses, so I will be with thee: I will not fail thee, nor forsake thee. **Be strong and of good courage:** *for unto this people shall thou divide an inheritance the land, which I sware unto their fathers to give them.* **Only be thou strong and very courageous, that thou mayest observe to do** *according to all the law, which Moses my servant commanded thee: turn not to the right hand or to the left, that thou mayest* **prosper withersoever thou goest.** *This book of the law shall not depart out of thy* **mouth;** *but thou shalt meditate therein day and night, that thou mayest observe to do according to all that is written therein: for then thou shalt make thy way prosperous, and then thou shalt have good success* (Joshua 1:5-8).

These verses point out that prosperity and success aren't going to come into our lives until we observe to do the Word of God. It takes courage to walk in faith obedience in a culture of disobedience. As humans, we love comfort and avoid confrontation, conflict, and opposition. I'm not condemning anyone for that. In the flesh, no one wants to be rejected or persecuted for their faith. I know that. God does too. That's why He told Joshua to meditate on Him in His Word day and night. That's why God tells us the same thing. God's Word meditated upon will make us strong and courageous in our faith obedience.

THE BRIDE OF CHRIST

What does the bride of Christ look like? What does it look like to be in union with Christ? We need to see in our hearts what that looks like. It looks like favor, victory, overcoming, always triumphing, glorious, righteous and truly holy, the salt of the earth (preserving the good and destroying the evil), winning! Just to name a few. It looks like forgiven and healed and sanctified to make a difference. We must learn and see ourselves the way God does: the bride of Jesus. God says meditating on these things will build courage to act on God's Word with a new or renewed attitude (perspective). Notice again Joshua 1:8:

> *This book of the law shall not depart out of your mouth: but thou shalt meditate therein day and night, that thou mayest observe to do according to all that is written therein: for then thou shalt make thy way prosperous, and thou shalt have good success.*

You won't do the Word of God if you are a wimp, and just hearing the Word won't reverse your wimpiness. If all you do is study it a little, and only hear God's Word occasionally, you will not have the courage to act on it. If you go back to your old way of thinking, seeing, and saying, you'll never mature in the things of God. If you don't put the Word in your heart and in your mouth, listen for the direction of the Holy Spirit, and stand on the Word regardless of what your eyes see or your feelings feel, you will be weak and defeated.

> We must learn and see ourselves the way God does: the bride of Jesus.

When you meditate on the Scriptures, when you talk to God and ask for wisdom, when you mutter His words under your breath and speak the commands of God out loud to your mountains, you will come to a point where the Word of God on the page has become flesh. It becomes an organic part of you, and God imparts the grace and courage to do it. Notice in 2 Peter 1:4 how God's Word changes us: *"And because of his glory and excellence, he has given us great and precious promises* [God's Word]. *These are the promises that enable you to share his divine nature and escape the world's corruption caused by human desires"* (NLT).

He made us promises, and through His promises, we become partakers of the divine nature. It's God's Word in our hearts and meditating on it that changes our lives and makes us Christlike (partakers of His divine nature). That is one of the promises of God that we can count on because God cannot lie; it is impossible (see Hebrews 6:18, Titus 1:2).

> When I stand on His Word, it builds my relationship with Him and changes me in the process.

You can be certain His promises are true. God's Word has the answer to any problem. When I stand on His Word, it builds my relationship with Him and changes me in the process. I'm not just memorizing Scriptures, but I'm drawing the life of the Word out by faith; I am conversing with God in prayer while I'm standing. The Holy Spirit is working in my heart to lead me to the truth of the Word in every situation, while changing my mind and life at the same time. It's a win-win deal!

THE BLESSED MAN

Blessed is the man that walketh not in the counsel of the ungodly, nor standeth in the way of sinners, nor sitteth in the seat of the scornful. But his delight is in the law of the Lord; and in his law doth he **meditate** *day and night. And he shall be like a tree planted by the rivers of water, that bringeth forth his fruit in its season; his leaf also shall not wither; and* **whatsoever he doeth shall prosper** *(*Psalm 1:1-3).

God is no respecter of persons (see Acts 10:34). All of His promises are yes and amen unto the glory of God by all of us (see 2 Corinthians 1:20). That is absolutely incredible when you really think about it. Through meditation on God and His Word, stability and success are a part of our everyday lives, regardless of our vocation. Meditating on our union with Christ and God's Word as it relates to our new condition in Christ (His bride) will bring about success in our lives. How can we have a bad day knowing we are married to Jesus and meditating on that versus our circumstances in this life? I really like how the The Message Bible words Psalm 1:1-2. *"How well God must like you—you don't hang out at Sin Saloon, you don't slink along Dead-End Road, you don't go to Smart-Mouth College. Instead you thrill to God's Word, you chew on Scripture day and night."*

How cool is that! "Sin Saloon," "slink along Dead-End Road," "go to Smart-Mouth College" (I love that one), "Chew on the Scripture day and night." That's what it means to meditate. We are chewing on our thoughts, so let those be God's thoughts. God's Word is His thoughts. When it comes to chewing on Scripture, we

OUR UNION WITH CHRIST

need to be like a cow. Cows have one stomach but multiple compartments. They get up in the morning and graze the field and all the grass goes into one compartment of the stomach. Then the cow finds a shade tree and burps (vomits!) it up. (Sorry for the visual, but that's how it works.) The cow chews everything all over again, which is called "chewing the cud." As the cow chews it the second time, the nutrients are released—all the vitamins and minerals come out of the grass and go into another compartment of the stomach. Then these digested nutrients are sent into the muscles, and that is what makes the meat become a great steak. Hallelujah! Can anyone say *prime rib?*

> Chewing on God's thoughts will bring the life of His thoughts into all areas of our lives.

A changed life comes from the nutrients that are released as we chew our "spiritual cud." As we feed on God's Word by hearing it and reading it, there will be a point where we meditate on what we've heard and read. That's when we are drawing the life out of what God has said. Chewing on God's thoughts will bring the life of His thoughts into all areas of our lives. Our will is affected, our emotions are healed, and our whole is becoming healthy as we are sustained and strengthened by divine nutrients of God's Word.

Green Things!

When I was a kid, my mother would cook and insist that I eat everything on my plate, including the green things. Now when I say *green things,* I'm not speaking in opposition to the color green or God's creativity with the different colors of food. Corn being yellow is great, red tomatoes, and white potatoes are wonderful. The color green in certain vegetables is very fine as well, and brown is my favorite color of all since it is the predominant color of meat! When I say *green things,* I'm referring to collard greens, mustard greens, turnip greens, spinach greens. Our family had a "THING" for these particular "GREEN THINGS," and we had them nearly every meal. My dad grew a garden, and it had all the different "greens" you could imagine. We lived in Orlando, Florida so this garden was nearly year-round, always producing more of those green things. Well, I didn't like them and struggled in my obedience to *"eat such things as are set before you"* (Luke 10:7)— one of the only scriptures my mom ever put on the fridge. I would eat the yellow, red, white, and especially the brown things but— ew—the green things.

"Why do I have to eat this stuff?" I asked. Even in my obedience I was struggling in my submission.

Mother basically said, "Duane, there are things in the green things that are not in the brown things."

"Yea, bad taste," I answered. My sharp wit and quick comebacks were traits not highly valued by my family.

My mom would continue her reasoning with, "There are vitamins and nutrients in them that when chewed and digested get all over your body." At the time that sounded a little spooky to me. The bottom line is, if the greens remained on the plate, they would not benefit my body. I had to chew them, digest them, and then what's in them got in me. In the same way, when you chew on the Word and digest it into your inner man, it gets all over your being and life.

Meditation is feeding on God's Word at a deeper, spiritual nutrient level than just hearing or reading. While those disciplines are vital to our relationship with the Lord, it's not until we meditate on what God is saying that we understand what He is saying; it helps us to embrace that word with all of our hearts, our mind, will, and emotions, which we are instructed to do (see Ezekiel 3:1-4, Revelation 10:8-11). Ezekiel and John both were commanded by God to *eat* the Word. How do you eat the Bible? In Matthew 4:4, Jesus refers to God's Word as bread. Peter refers to God's Word as milk and as we receive it we will grow (see 1 Peter 2:2). We eat it by meditating on it and chewing on it in our thoughts.

HARD SAYING

*And Jesus said to them, I assure you, most solemnly I tell you, you cannot have any life in you unless **you eat the flesh of the Son of man** and drink his blood [unless you appropriate His life and saving merit of His blood]* (John 6:53 AMPC).

This was one of Jesus' most controversial teachings. Many of His disciples left Him over it. It sounded like a reference to cannibalism and many did not understand the metaphor. Just like food is essential to our natural life, Jesus is saying that faith is like feeding on who Jesus is; it will sustain us in our newly found life in Christ, engrafted to Him. Jesus is to our hearts what food is to our bodies. Meditation is an act of faith. It is God interacting with our thoughts and emotions and God renewing our minds from within to transform our lives. I'm eating His flesh and drinking His blood when I receive by faith all He provided for me at the cross in the sacrificing of His body and the shedding of His blood. I can't encourage you enough in this rhythm of grace in your life. What we meditate on affects every single part of our life. What we are meditating on becomes our dominate thoughts, pictures, and emotions driving our hearts and lives.

TWO MINDS (CARNAL OR SPIRITUAL)

We are called to quiet ourselves and ponder what God has said about us. There are only two thought tracks to run on (no third rail), and both tracks have a destination. Romans 8:6 says *"...to be carnally minded is death; but to be spiritually minded is life and peace."* That is the power of our thoughts, and even what we unconsciously think on in the "back of our minds" is mediation of sorts. The power of the Christian life doesn't come from the mind, but it does come *through* it. Meditation is me discovering and agreeing with what God thinks. We either are choosing carnal thoughts (destruction, forms of death) or spiritual thoughts (victory, forms of life and peace).

> Jesus is to our hearts what food is to our bodies.

My thought life is connected to my faith walk. Your mind and what you do with it really matters. You have to see Christ's work on the cross in you to experience life and peace. That comes through meditation on God's Word day and night. God actually keeps us in perfect peace when our minds are stayed on Him and we trust Him (see Isaiah 26:3).

NO WORRIES

Always be full of joy in the Lord. I say it again— rejoice! Let everyone see that you are considerate in all you do. Remember, the Lord is coming soon. **Don't worry about anything; instead, pray about everything.** *Tell God what you need, and thank him for all he has done. Then you will experience God's peace, which exceeds anything we can understand. His peace will guard your hearts and minds as you live in Christ Jesus* (Philippians 4:4-7 NLT).

When we pray and thank God, the peace of God in our spirits will guard our hearts and minds. If we choose to meditate on our problems, then anxiety will infiltrate how we live. But if we choose to pray and focus on Jesus as the true and trusted Rescuer, then peace is released and dominates how we live. These are Paul's final instructions after we've prayed. *"And now, dear brothers and sisters, one final thing. Fix your thoughts on what is true, and honorable, and right, and pure, and lovely, and admirable. Think about things that are excellent and worthy of praise. Keep putting into practice all you learned and received from me—everything you heard from me and saw me doing. Then the God of peace will be with you"* (Philippians 4:8-9 NLT).

We can have both "peace with God" and "the God of peace" in our lives. Peace with God comes through faith in the blood of Jesus shed for our sins. The God of peace comes through setting our minds on Him. In these verses, Paul has laid out how to deal with worry and anxiety with prayer and thanksgiving. In verse 8, he gives the final instructions for experiencing peace in our soul and our lives. He tell us to fix our thoughts on certain things and set our minds like a cruise control on our cars.

Here is a list, if you will, of some thought tracks to travel: what is true, honorable and right, pure, lovely, admirable, excellent, and worthy of praise, think on these (see Philippians 4:8). These all point to our union with Christ and our new condition as His bride. We may feel like a dropped date at the prom or nothing worthy of admiration. Yet Jesus has changed our lives and what God's Word says about who we are (bride) is true, honorable and right, pure, lovely, admirable, excellent and our husband is worthy of all praise.

While I don't believe this is an exhaustive list of thought tracks, it would be exhausting for some Christians to go a whole day lining up their thought choices with this list. The world of darkness trains us to think the opposite of this list. The renewing of our minds involves paying attention to our patterns of thinking. It requires rhythms of grace that include purposely setting aside time to meditate, speak the Word, sing the Word, talk to your spouse about the Word, write down the Word, and stick it up where you see it frequently as you go about your busy day. It takes effort to form new habits. That is why these actions are called disciplines.

I'm not suggesting legalism or any work of law, but a work of faith involves setting my mind on the God of grace. When Moses went up on Mt. Sinai to receive the Ten Commandments, he provided the stone tablets. Then God wrote on them with His own finger. Look at the terms of the new covenant and God's role in mind renewal. *"But this is the new covenant I will make with the people of Israel on that day, says the Lord: I will put my laws in their minds, and I will write them on their hearts. I will be their God, and they will be my people"* (Hebrews 8:10 NLT).

Think of your brain in terms of two hemispheres (tablets). One hemisphere is the mind (thoughts, opinions, images) and the other is your heart (feelings, emotions). God has promised to write His Word on our minds and hearts. WOW! Our two tablets simply need to be given to God in meditation, and God will renew them which will result in changing our lives. God is actually the One who renews our minds; we just yield them to Him in prayer and meditation. God changes how we think when we give Him what we think on. God changes how we feel in our emotions when we share them with Him in prayer and meditation. Remember when we meditate, we are muttering (speaking). Check this out! *"My heart is overflowing with a good theme; I recite my composition concerning the King; my tongue is the pen of a ready writer"* (Psalm 45:1 NKJV).

> Learning to set your thoughts on God's love for you and refusing to allow them to stray, causes faith in God to work.

The words we choose to speak are the pen of a ready writer. I believe God takes the words we speak and imprints them on our minds and hearts. In meditation we mutter God's Word, and God is committed to writing His thoughts on the tablet of our hearts. As we simply pray about whatever is troubling us, practice the discipline of setting our minds on Him, and speak His Word, He changes our paradigms. Old thought tracks begin to be dug up, and new thought tracks begin to be laid. Learning to set your thoughts on God's love for you and refusing to allow them to stray, causes faith in God to work. I do not judge God's love for me by circumstances or emotions but rather by the cross and what Scripture declares as truth. Chew on it!

One of the most powerful statements and principles in all of Scripture is found in Genesis 11 and the account of the Tower of Babel. God had flooded the earth in righteous judgment to preserve the righteous seed (Noah and his family) to get Jesus the Messiah in the earth to save us all. The earth was being populated again through Noah's family, and men's hearts were being manipulated by sin (Satan) once again. In an effort to avoid God's judgment ever again, they endeavored to build a tower and city for their own glory.

> *And the LORD came down to see the city and the tower, which the children of men builded. And the LORD said, Behold, the people is one, and they have all one language; and this they begin to do: and **now nothing will be restrained from them, which they have imagined to do** (Genesis 11:5-6).*

They were of one language and words mattered. Nothing they imagined to do would be restrained from them. There was power in imagination even for an evil cause. What can God do with a positive imagination for a good cause? If we can see it and say it, then we can have it. What we see and say needs to line up with God's will and plan for our lives. That is what meditation is all about. We train our minds to see what God sees and we say in prayer what God says. Most never spend enough time with God to see and say what God sees and says. Once we see it and say it, nothing will be restrained from us that God wills for our lives. See yourself united to Christ. Imagine the benefits and blessings of marrying Jesus. The beautiful positive images of God's love for us are endless.

CHAPTER 15

GOD IS LOVE

*And this is life eternal, that they might **know thee** the only true God, and **Jesus Christ**, whom thou has sent.*
—JOHN 17:3

Knowing God changes everything. To know God means we begin a journey into the contents and wonders of His heart. The holy love that Jesus has for us as His bride has no equal or rival. His love is revealed progressively from glory to greater glory as we grow in the knowledge of Him as our husband.

> The holy love that Jesus has for us as His bride has no equal or rival.

Through our ever-increasing knowledge of Him, our love for each other continues to increase as well. In Ephesians 3 Paul writes a beautiful prayer for us, *"And to know the love of Christ, which passeth knowledge, that ye might be filled with all the fullness of God"* (Ephesians 3:19).

How is it possible to know something beyond knowledge? That sounds like a mystery, a great mystery. How do we experience God's fullness? It is only by revelation knowledge of God's love for us that we begin to experience His fullness in our lives. It's a revelation of how much He loves us that cannot be comprehended or understood with our carnal, unrenewed minds or our five senses.

As I come to know the love that Jesus has for me, I am continually filled by Him. I looked in the mirror today and saw some of my Husband's qualities. As each day passes, I continue to see more of Him than the day before. This is how I know that I'm growing in my knowing of His love. The more I come to know Him, the more there is to know and enjoy. That is what Paul is referring to when he talks about the knowing that surpasses all knowledge. It will take ages for God to show us the exceeding riches of His grace and kindness toward us in our Husband, Jesus (Ephesians 2:6-7). The knowing by revelation began when we made Jesus Lord of our life, but it will continue beyond our natural lives. It amazes me to think that the revealed knowledge of God never ends and is never exhausted.

> As I come to know the love that Jesus has for me, I am continually filled by Him.

His love cannot be known or understood by natural, sense knowledge (what we see, smell, taste, hear, or feel). It cannot be discerned by our circumstances. Many people judge God's love for them based on their situation, especially when their situation is a negative one. That leads to confusion and disillusionment because each situation is affected by many different factors which may not involve God's love at all. We can only know the love of God when it is revealed to us by the Holy Spirit. The more we know and experience His love, the more we will experience His life and power too!

When I tell people how much Jesus loves them, there seems to be somewhat of a disconnect. In many cases I hear, "So what!" or "I know it!" but it really means nothing to them. I believe it is because we use the word *love* to express such a broad range of emotions and perspectives that it has become meaningless and descriptive of nothing. Phrases like "I love ice cream!" "I love my job!" "I love this!" "I love that!" waters down people's ability to comprehend and be affected by God's love for us. I've had people speak of loving their dog and wife in the same conversation. I hope we all know there is a different kind of love for our dog than our wife. Help us, Jesus! The apostle John reveals the uniqueness of God's kind of love in these verses in First John 3:1-3.

> *Behold, what manner of love the Father hath bestowed upon us, that we should be called the sons of God: therefore the world knoweth us not, because it knew him not. Beloved, now are we the sons of God, and it doth not yet appear what we shall be: but we know that, when he shall appear, we shall be like him; for we shall see him as he is. And every man that hath this hope in him purifieth himself, even as he is pure.*

John asks, "What manner of love is this?" In other words, what kind of love changes us from enemies of God to children of God? What kind of love changes us inside in our spirit man so we are "married to Jesus"? It's as if this love is out of place in our dark world. Like a rose blossoming in the desert, it certainly stands out and demands our attention.

GOD IS LOVE...NO REALLY!

*Whosoever shall confess that Jesus is the Son of God, God dwelleth in him, and he in God. And we have known and believed the love that God hath to us. **God is love; and he that dwelleth in love dwelleth in God, and God in him. Herein is our love made perfect, that we may have boldness in the day of judgment: because as he is, so are we in this world** (1 John 4:15-17).*

You cannot separate God from love or love from God as so many try to do today. They call things love that are contrary to God Himself. First John 4:8 also declares, *"God is love."* He doesn't just *have* love for us, but He *is* love *to* us. Could this be true that God loves me in this manner? God doesn't just "have" love for you and me, for that would suggest a limit. If you "have" something, you can have less or more of that something. It can be measured and bottled; it has some kind of boundary or can be contained somehow. If you have water, then you can have more or less water than your neighbor. But if you are H20, then you are who you are, without variation or degree. God doesn't *have* love for you or me; He *is* love to us—without variation or degree.

UNCONDITIONAL LOVE

We don't earn or merit God's love. We can't do enough good for Him to love us more—that would be conditional love. And we cannot do enough bad to get Him to love us less—that would also be conditional love. He loves us with a perfect, infinite, unconditional love because love is who He is. His love for us is based on His nature and character, not our conduct or performance. That's why His love never changes—because He never changes. First John 4:17 declares our love is made perfect when we see that He is love from eternity past to eternity future—boundless, unlimited, all-consuming. It's in only seeing and believing God's love for me that I am now able to love myself and others.

"Love is of God." It is not of me, my flesh or this world. I cannot love with God's love in and of myself. It's not a warm and fuzzy feeling or fantastical reveries emanating from my carnality. And it is definitely not self-centered or selfish. Nothing in our natural man will cut it. I can't drum up "love and peace" toward others, even if I live in a commune and speak only soft, special, nice words, and espouse world peace. I can only love others with the measure of God's love I have received for myself. I can't give what I don't have. I must receive God's kindness, His manner of love, for me. Then I am able to love anyone else with that kind of love.

HOW TO GROW IN TRUE LOVE

Two things have to be in place in order for us to love as God originally ordained for you and me to love. *"Beloved, let us love one another: for love is of God; and everyone that loveth is born of God, and knoweth God"* (1 John 4:7).

1. We must be "born of God."

This means we accept Jesus' marriage proposal, so to speak. It is impossible to love one another as God desires when we are coming from a fallen condition in Adam. But Jesus does beckon us and to be born again means we say yes to Him as Lord. We must be born again by the Word and Spirit of God to even begin to have the capacity to love. We must experience the forgiveness of our sins and live in the reality that we are not our old selves anymore—we are a new creation. We must believe with all our heart God raised Jesus from the dead and confess Him as Lord (see Romans 10:9-10).

2. We must "know God."

It is in our relationship with Jesus, as in a marriage, that the love of God is shed abroad in our hearts by the Holy Spirit (see Romans 5:5). Notice how John says it: *"He that loveth not knoweth not God; for God is love"* (1 John 4:8).

When we don't love, it's because we don't know God. He didn't say that if we don't love each other, we are not born of God and don't know God at all. He said our lack of love one for another is because we are not growing in our knowing of God's love for us.

I know many good Christian people who are born again and do not walk in love as God has ordained for us to do. They, through the new creation, have the ability by God to love with His love, but they simply have not matured. And much of this is because they do not know even the shallowest depth of God's love for them. When you speak with them, you can see and feel that they may be a convert, but they are not a disciple. Their marriage to Jesus is as shallow and superficial as many domestic marriages we see today. Disciples are ever growing in their knowing of Jesus. They are developing the marriage relationship where they are receiving the love Jesus has for them and overflowing with the power, gentleness, wisdom, and patience of God's love toward everyone they encounter. As we grow in our knowledge of *who* and *what* love is, we expand our desire and ability to love unconditionally and to express God's love in every kind of relationship we encounter.

ACTION VS. FEELING

God showed how much he loved us by sending His one and only Son into the world so that we might have eternal life through him. This is real love—not that we love God, but that he loved us and sent his Son as a sacrifice to take away our sins (1 John 4:9-10 NLT).

God loved us in action, not feelings and emotions. He initiated sending Jesus to us, and Jesus was faithful in performing an impossibly selfless act—dying on the cross for the sins of the world. We did not love God and then He loved us back. *"We love Him because He first loved us"* (1 John 4:19).

> Disciples are ever growing in their knowing of Jesus.

Jesus' sacrifice came out of His character and nature, not a response to any merit on our part. There was nothing in any of us worth loving or deserving of God's love. That's a different kind of love. God loved us first, and then we responded to His love. We could not love God, ourselves, or anyone else until we received God's love for us. Love is of God, not us or this world, nor my emotions and flesh.

NO FEAR IN LOVE

*There is no fear in love; but **perfect love casteth out fear**: because fear hath torment. He that feareth is not made perfect in love* (1 John 4:18).

God's undeserved love casts out fear. All forms of fear are cast out when we *know* and receive His love. If you have any fear of anything or anybody, you are coming up short on knowing God's perfect love. You may know it to a measure, but any existing fear reveals a need to be growing in your knowledge of His heart and purpose. I'm not saying this to condemn anyone, but I want to convince you that seeking God and His love for you will help you. It is impossible to fear if you are abiding in God's love for you that is displayed in your heavenly Husband Jesus. A fear of man cannot remain when you're standing in the loving arms of Jesus.

RELIGIOUS FEAR

The biggest fear I've been delivered from is religious fear. I had a fear of God's wrath and curses coming on me if I failed in anyway. Under religious fear, it is very easy to almost automatically live under the shadow of guilt and condemnation. A very prominent fear is found in how we think people view us, or judge us, and especially how our enemies seem to have the power to ensnare us. Often this fear is well-manifested in competitive work situations or politics. In some countries, there is the very terrible fear of imprisonment or death because of faith in Jesus or His Word. Any sort of fear is truly an enemy to us, but in Luke God speaks very directly concerning this. He wills that we serve Him as His bride

"...without fear, in holiness and righteousness before Him all the days of our life" (Luke 1:74-75).

There is a fear of God that is a biblical, healthy, reverential fear. Jesus operated, as well as all the prophets, in the fear of the Lord (see Isaiah 11:2-3). The fear of the Lord is not being afraid of God. It is not a tormenting fear of His rejecting or punishing you at any moment. It is a "fear" that speaks of tremendous respect and obedience. God has not given us a demonic or tormenting kind of fear, but He has given us a spirit of power, love, and a sound mind (see 2 Timothy 1:7).

> If you have any fear of anything or anybody, you are coming up short on knowing God's perfect love.

What husband wants a relationship with a wife that is afraid of him? While he wants respect (fear of the Lord), he doesn't want her living in a state of quaking fear of rejection, ready to duck some emotional blow to the center of her being. Jesus in our marriage relationship is not condemning us or wishing any ill will toward us. He wants us as His bride to be free from any fear, worry, or condemnation.

NO CONDEMNATION

*There is therefore now **no condemnation** to them which are in Christ Jesus, who walk not after the flesh, but after the Spirit. For the law of the Spirit of life in Christ Jesus hath made me free from the law of sin and death. For what the law could not do, in that it was* *weak through the flesh, God sending his own Son in the likeness of sinful flesh, and for sin, condemned sin in the flesh: That the righteousness of the law might be fulfilled in us, who walk not after the flesh, but after the Spirit* (Romans 8:1-4).

Jesus takes care of the enemies of fear and condemnation. He did for us what we could never do. He kept the law. Then He paid for what we did breaking the law. Jesus was raised from the dead to accomplish through our faith what the law could never do through our works—make us righteous. Because of our fallen nature, we never would have been able to keep the law of the Old Testament. We were always transgressing and breaking the law. So, He died a horrible death on the cross to take our penalty, as a husband would lay down his life for the wife of His youth. Verse 3 says He was condemned in His flesh for all our sins. God judged all our sins in the flesh of Jesus (see 1 Peter 2:24). What manner of love is this? This manner of love casts all fear out! No fear of wrath, curses, punishment or rejection (see Galatians 3:13). This is God's love for you and me!

HOW DO I KNOW GOD'S LOVE?

1. Jesus loved us in offering Himself for our sins (Romans 8:1-4).

He loved us enough to take our place and suffer on our behalf. Jesus commands me to love my wife with the same love He had for me at the cross. This is why I never make a big deal out of Sue submitting to me, because I am to love her with a love that is not of me but of God. My loving her seems to be a more serious imperative and a larger task than her submitting. The loving command is much more challenging than the submitting command (see Ephesians 5:25).

2. Jesus loves us as He does Himself (Ephesians 5:29).

Let that sink in. Jesus has a wholesome, healthy self-love. He loves us with the same love He has for Himself. In other words, He is at peace with Himself, and He is at peace with us. We are a part of His body. He loves His own body and would never put sickness or disease on His own body. He would never abuse His own body, and neither will He do that to you or me, His wife.

3. He displays His love by nourishing us (Ephesians 5:29).

To nourish means to supply what is necessary for life, health, and growth. Jesus does nothing but promote our well-being. He never pushes us down but constantly lifts us up. He never uses His authority over us as a husband for destruction; He uses it for edification (see 2 Corinthians 10:8).

> God's love for us is revealed in Jesus and the cross.

4. He cherishes us (Ephesians 5:29).

To cherish means to have a person in the forefront of your mind, seek out ways to do good things for them, treat them as dear and special, care for them tenderly, and cling to them fondly. Jesus has nothing but happy thoughts toward you and me. Years ago, I was preaching and I heard the Lord speak to me about how I was addressing His wife. My tone was not proper. I was being too harsh and unkind. My preaching has never been the same since then. What if we treated one another as if we were the Lord's wife? What if we spoke to one another knowing it would get back to Him?

God's love for us is revealed in Jesus and the cross. It is actually taught by the Holy Spirit, not caught by an emotion. In the next chapter, we will see what God's love looks like and how it is defined and described.

CHAPTER 16

LOVE IS TAUGHT
NOT CAUGHT

*But as touching brotherly love ye need not that I write unto
you: for ye yourselves are taught of God to love one another.*
—1 Thessalonians 4:9

Once, during a marriage seminar I was holding, I felt impressed to
look at First Corinthians 13:1-8 and share on God's love. I taught
on God's love and what it looks like in a healthy marriage. We
don't fall into and out of God's kind of love. It's not like a mood
that comes and goes. It never fluctuates. And it is not "outside of
us," just swooping in and overtaking our thinking and emotions.
God's love is also not like a virus or cold that comes and goes with
no rhyme or reason.

Love is modeled by Jesus, by good parents, grandparents, leaders, teachers, and shop clerks. There are no cupids shooting arrows
into your heart. We learn it. It was a surprise to many in attendance at the seminar that love was taught, not caught. In Titus 2:4,

Paul encourages the older women to *"teach the young women to be sober, to love their husbands, to love their children."*

WOW!

Young women need to be taught how to love their husbands and children by those with godly experience. Young men need to be taught by older, wiser men as well. Young men don't automatically know how to love a wife and how to love their children, especially if they had difficult fathers or no father at all. I used to think that you either love someone or you don't. Well, I thought wrong. While love affects our emotions

> While love affects our emotions and feelings, they are not the source for or of love—God is!

and feelings, they are not the source for or of love—God is! He teaches us how to love.

When our children come to us and ask how to know when they are in love or have love for someone, we can answer the question through the Scripture (see 1 Corinthians 13). Love is taught and defined in God's Word both living (Jesus and the cross) and written (the Scriptures). As a father of four, I had to navigate through these alligator- and snake-infested waters (it felt like that anyway) with my own children. I had to constantly share the character traits of love versus the enticement of lust or fading infatuation, paying attention to an unselfish, caring demeanor versus a selfish desire or need for self-gratification. When a boy says he loves someone, nine out of ten times she has been drinking milk, and it has done her body good (Let that sink in!). When a girl says she is in love, that infatuation disappears when he abuses her or he decides to move on.

DEER IN THE HEADLIGHTS

Because we, as parents, many times don't know how to explain true love, we say things we really don't believe or mean. A child will ask, "How do I know I'm in love?" and we answer, "Well, uh... you'll just know."

They come back two weeks later and say, "Guess what Mom and Dad! I'm in love with so and so."

Then we say, "Oh, no, you're not!"

And they say, "You told me I would just know, and I'm telling you that I know. Now you're saying I don't know!?" It's maddening for both parties. But what if it could be explained and defined once and for all what love is? What does it look like or act like?

GOD'S LOVE

God's kind of love in time can profoundly affect feelings but feelings are not the source of love. While I'm using the King James translation, I've replaced the word *charity* with *love*. *Charity* literally means "acts of benevolence or love." God's love involves the assent of the will (choice) in matters of principle, duty, or propriety, regardless of feelings in the moment.

> *Love suffereth long, and is kind; love envieth not: love vaunteth not itself, is not puffed up, Doth not behave itself unseemly, seeketh not her own, is not easily provoked, thinketh no evil; Rejoiceth not in iniquity, but rejoiceth in the truth; Beareth all things, believeth all*

things, hopeth all things, endureth all things. Love never faileth. (1 Corinthians 13:4-8).

This passage specifies sixteen character traits of love. These are definitive manifestations of love. This is what God's love looks like:

1. Love is long-suffering (patient)
2. Love is kind (gentle and merciful)
3. Love doesn't envy (possessive of what is another's)
4. Love isn't boastful (cocky or conceited)
5. Love is not proud (not self-centered on me, myself, and I)
6. Love doesn't behave itself unseemly (isn't rude or disrespectful)
7. Love seeks not its own (isn't self-seeking)
8. Love is not easily provoked (is slow to get offended and not touchy)
9. Love thinks no evil (doesn't meditate on another's faults)
10. Love never rejoices in iniquity (or happy at others falling or failing)
11. Love rejoices in the truth (not offended by truth but celebrates it)
12. Love bears all things (it carries our burdens)
13. Love believes all things (it has faith in us and believes the best of others)

14. Love hopes all things (it sees our end at our beginning)
15. Love endures all things (in all circumstances)
16. Love never fails (it lasts forever, is not in and out, and never stops)

Very little, if any, of that list involves our emotions, at least in the way most explain love. Emotions are mentioned but not like the world means when it refers to love. In the world, lust and love are used interchangeably. What the world calls love is very harmful and, in some cases, hateful to our neighbor. Although they can involve strong emotions, adultery and sexual perversions are not love. *"Love worketh no ill to his neighbor: therefore love is the fulfilling of the law"* (Romans 13:10).

> Love is not just what I do—as in being kind—but it also includes what I don't do.

Love is not just what I do—as in being kind—but it also includes what I don't do. If it works ill toward my fellow man, then it is not love. You may think you love another man's wife, but do you love her husband? Do you love her children? Do you think you are working ill toward any of them? When Paul prayed for the Christians in Philippi, he prayed their love would abound more and more *"in knowledge and all judgment"* (Philippians 1:9).

Notice that we need love to abound in knowledge (taught to love) and in all judgment (discernment). As I was teaching these sixteen character traits of love, the Lord told me that this is how He relates to us as His wife. This is how God relates to us in our covenant marriage relationship. This is what it looks like to be loved by Jesus.

1. Jesus is patient.

He is not upset all the time, wishing I would get my act together. He is constantly developing me and helps me to get through my stubborn immaturity. Even while He is longing for the harvest of the world, He has His eye on the prize, and He has His eye on us, His wife. He truly is long-suffering. Knowing God's patience with me has allowed me to work through my shortcomings and run to the Lord versus from the Lord. We are told in Scripture it is *"through faith and patience"* we inherit God's promises (Hebrew 6:12). Jesus through faith and patience with me will inherit the promise of a bride (the Church) without spot or wrinkle (mature).

2. Jesus is kind.

The Lord's kindness and tender mercies are fresh and new every morning. In Psalm 23:6, the Word declares that *"Surely goodness and mercy shall follow me all the days of my life."* Psalm 103:4 declares that God *"crowns you with lovingkindness and tender mercies"* (NKJV). Psalm 42:8 states that God commands His loving-kindness over us in the daytime. His love is shown in kindness, and mercy is a part of His kindness. Hebrews 8:12 outlines one of the many covenant promises God makes with us in the new covenant relationship we have with Jesus. *"...For I will be merciful to their unrighteousness, and their sins and their iniquities will I remember no more."* While God's love for me doesn't ignore sin, God is merciful toward me in my failings and shortcomings. He is not angry or wrathful toward me in regard to sin. Because of His kindness, I can overcome sin and break out of its enslaving power.

"For sin shall not have dominion over you: for ye are not under the law, but under grace" (Romans 6:14). Kindness is a part of God's grace that breaks sin's dominion.

3. Jesus doesn't envy.

To envy is to have a feeling of discontent or covetousness with regard to another's advantage, success, or possessions. Jesus delights and rejoices in our success and prosperity. We are a reflection of Jesus' husbandly. We are not a beaten-down, oppressed wife; we are a celebrated wife. He willingly shares in His victory over sin and

> We are a reflection of Jesus' husbandly.

Satan. As we share in His sufferings, we also share in His glory (see Romans 8:17-18). He actually finds pleasure in our prosperity: *"Let them shout for joy and be glad, Who favor my righteous cause; And let them say continually, "Let the Lord be magnified, Who has pleasure in the prosperity of His servant"* (Psalm 35:27 NKJV).

4. Jesus isn't boastful, loud, self-promoting, or self-exalting.

He doesn't draw attention to Himself. *"Come unto me, all ye that labour and are heavy laden, and I will give you rest. Take my yoke upon you, and learn of me; for I am meek and lowly in heart: and ye shall find rest unto your souls"* (Matthew 11:28-29). While Jesus calls us unto Himself, He is not full of Himself.

Jesus is meek and lowly in heart. He is humble! Few people understand the humility of Jesus, who was God made flesh. What kind of humility did it take for deity to enter humanity? This is how Jesus loved us. He became one of us and identified with our humanity so we can now identify with Him. He identified with the old creation in Adam so we could identify with the new creation in Him.

5. Jesus is not proud and puffed up.

Pride is simply self-centeredness. *Believe it or not, it is not all about Him.* We want to be devoted, so we say, "Jesus, Jesus, Jesus. It's all about Jesus." I know that's how we've been conditioned, but He really thinks about you and me much more than Himself. If all He ever thought about was Himself, why did He go to the cross and die for you and me? We were the joy set before Him that caused Him to endure the cross (see Hebrews 12:2). He really is thinking about you and me and it is always happy thoughts!

6. Jesus is not rude.

He doesn't act unseemly. He will never embarrass or shame us in any way. He never "dresses us down" in public. While love corrects and chastens us (see Hebrews 12:6-7), God doesn't uncover us in our mistakes. *"Above all things have intense and unfailing love for one another, for love covers a multitude of sins [forgives and disregards the offenses of others]* (1 Peter 4:8 AMPC).

When I say He doesn't uncover our sin, I do not mean He covers it up. It means He does not uncover us with ill will or intent to hurt or damage. We can trust Him in our relationship. While He helps me with overcoming sin, He never uncovers my nakedness.

7. Jesus is not self-seeking.

Jesus seeks not His own. It's not "His way or the highway." I know this must sound strange to many of us. Our idea of God, painted by dead religion, is not one of love. Many of us think God almost couldn't care less about our hurts and pains. Many falsely accuse God of such unseemly behavior. In reality, Jesus is watching out for us. He is constantly thinking of our well-being. *"Who is he that condemneth? It is Christ that died, yea rather, that is risen again, who is even at the right hand of God, who also maketh intercession for us"* (Romans 8:34). He is thinking of us and praying for us. He is constantly thinking of our good and not harm.

8. Jesus is not easily provoked.

He doesn't fly off the handle with anger. Boy, that's a different description of God than the one I came up under! I thought He was continually angry with me and frustrated with all my failures. I thought He was never happy or pleased with anything about me, because I was sure that no matter what I did, it was never going to be good enough. What a terrible husband that would be. What a terrible marriage that would be. Jesus has made peace with us through His blood shed at the cross (see Colossians 1:20). God has made a covenant of peace with us: *"For this is as the waters of Noah unto me: for as I have sworn that the waters of Noah should no more go over the earth; so have I sworn that I would not be wroth with thee, nor rebuke thee. For the mountains shall depart, and the hills be removed; but my kindness shall not depart from thee, neither shall the covenant of my peace be removed, saith the Lord that hath mercy on thee"* (Isaiah 54:9-10).

Our warfare with God has ended. God is no longer angry with us. What Jesus did on the cross for our sins was more than enough. We have been fully pardoned, and God is pleased with us because of Jesus and our faith in His love. *"Comfort, yes, comfort*

My people!' Says your God. 'Speak comfort to Jerusalem, and cry out to her, That her warfare is ended, That her iniquity is pardoned; For she has received from the Lord's hand double for all her sins'" (Isaiah 40:1-2 NKJV). God's not angry or mad at us, so why are so many mad at Him? Maybe they don't know how much He loves them.

9. Jesus thinks no evil.

He doesn't sit around and think ugly things about His marriage to the Church. Jesus sees the good in us and the success of His finished work on the cross. Remember, He sees Himself in us. *"For I know the thoughts that I think toward you, saith the Lord, thoughts of peace, and not of evil, to give you an expected end"* (Jeremiah 29:11).

God knows His thoughts toward us and they are all happy thoughts. We need to renew our minds to His thoughts toward us. He sees you and me as *"...bone of my bones, and flesh of my flesh..."* (Genesis 2:23). He looks at the good in our spirit not the bad in our flesh.

> God knows His thoughts toward us and they are all happy thoughts.

He doesn't hold our sins over our heads. He doesn't bring up our past mistakes and lord them over us. He is not keeping count of how many times we have fallen or failed. He is not condemning or shaming us for our mistakes. He thinks no evil.

10. Jesus never rejoices in iniquities or injustice.

He'll never cheer over our shortcomings or failures. He will only say, "Come on, get up! You can do it. I will help you. Come on, I love you, and I am here for you." He comforts us in our shortcomings and flaws rather than condemn us (see Isaiah 40:1-2). He never rejoices over us failing or others failing us. We are told in Scripture that a *"just man falleth seven times, and riseth up again"* (Proverbs 24:16). We are able to get up again because we know Jesus doesn't rejoice in our falling but rather in our getting back up. *"The Lord thy God in the midst of thee is mighty; he will save, he will rejoice over thee with joy; he will rest in his love, he will joy over thee with singing"* (Zephaniah 3:17). He is at rest with His love for us, and we need to be at rest in His kind of love for us.

11. Jesus rejoices in the truth.

He rejoices every time we see the truth and act in accordance with it. He is our cheerleader (see Zephaniah 3:17). *"For I rejoiced greatly, when the brethren came and testified of the truth that is in thee, even as thou walkest in the truth. **I have no greater joy than to hear that my children walk in truth**"* (3 John 3-4). Why would Jesus take so much joy in us seeing and walking in truth? It is truth and knowing the truth that brings a greater freedom in our lives to serve the Lord. The only way faith comes is by hearing God's Word (see Romans 10:17), and the Word is truth (see John 17:17). Remember it is impossible to please God without faith. Before I understood the great mystery, I tried to please God in self-effort. I tried to be good enough, work hard enough, start enough and quit enough to be accepted and loved by the Lord. One day, I discovered that everything I was trying to become, I actually already was in Christ. Through my union with Christ I was made righteous and truly holy (see Romans 5:19, 2 Corinthians 5:21). The truth of my new condition in Christ brought true liberty and freedom, causing me to rest in His love.

12. Jesus bears all things.

He is our steadfast supporter. He wants us to trust Him and cast all our cares on Him for He cares for us. The apostle Peter encourages us to *"Pour out all your worries and stress upon him and leave them there, for he always tenderly cares for you"* (1 Peter 5:7 TPT). Jesus as our steadfast husband doesn't want us to carry worry, anxiety, or stress. He knows these things can make His Word of non-effect in our lives (see Mark 4:18-19). We are not created to carry burdens; He does that for us. Part of yielding and submitting as His wife is to trust Him to carry us and our burdens as we go through this life. We all need to learn to "let it go."

13. Jesus believes all positive things.

He believes in us even when we doubt Him. He sees our potential as His faithful, loving bride. Think for a moment of what Paul said to a young pastor Timothy as it relates to Jesus and His belief in us. *"If we believe not, yet he abideth faithful: He cannot deny himself"* (2 Timothy 2:13). Wow! When we waver, He does not. When we (and we all do) go through a faith crisis, He is not shaken.

Notice how He cannot deny Himself. We are united to Him in a way of being flesh of His flesh, bone of His bones. He cannot deny us any more than Himself because we are a part of Him. We are married to Him now (one Spirit). It's so good to know He believes in me when I'm not sure I do at times. I've doubted myself so many times, but never Him.

14. Jesus hopes all things.

He sees and declares our end at our beginning (see Isaiah 46:10). He has begun a good work in us and will finish it (see

Philippians 1:6). Hope is a powerful force in our lives. We can live around forty days without food before starvation really sets in, and we can go without water for about three to four days. Yet we can't live one day without hope. That's how powerful hope is in our lives. Jesus never losses hope in the coming of the new heaven and earth wherein righteousness will reign. The hope of the resurrection and all things being restored and the Kingdom manifesting on this earth is all a part of our union with Jesus that He has for us and Him together throughout eternity.

15. Jesus endures all things.

This is immensely comforting. He endures our falling and confusion. Divorce is never an option in our covenant relationship. I'm so grateful He hates divorce and is in it for the long haul. His steadfast love for us is reassuring (see Malachi 2:16). I know if I was Jesus, I would have given up on me at least a time or two (okay... maybe more). It didn't say He endures some things, most things, or a few things. It says "all things." Jesus is not a fair-weather lover in our marriage together. He didn't commit to our union as long as I step it up and fulfill my end of the bargain. When I got saved, Jesus entered our marriage covenant for better or worse, richer or poorer, and in sickness and health until death brings us face to face in heaven. *"To be absent from the body, and to be present with the Lord"* (2 Corinthians 5:8).

16. Jesus never fails.

He will always be there to walk us through any circumstance. We may fail but He won't. Everyone in Scripture has failed, and everyone I know, including me, has failed. Jesus is the only person in human history who has not! We are married to someone who has never failed, never been wrong, never missed it! While that can seem intimidating to someone like me who has failed enough to be considered skilled at it, I can put my trust in Him. Me knowing, in true humility, my weaknesses and shortcomings actually has driven me to a Husband who never fails. Over the years I've come to trust Him instead of myself (see Proverbs 3:5)

> What a witness we can be to the world being happily married to Jesus.

These sixteen character traits are who Jesus is and how He relates to us in His love. There is no wrath, anger, curse, or rejection in our union with Christ. We have total acceptance and a love based on His character, not our conduct. His love is a love that will never give in, give up, or give out on us.

CONCLUSION

What a great mystery! Our marriage to Jesus produces a changed life in which we bear much fruit and a relationship with Jesus where we are best friends in union with each other bringing glory to the heavenly Father. What a witness we can be to the world being happily married to Jesus. What force for good God has for us, united to the Light of the world in holy matrimony. It is such a blessing to live from a

> But the Christian has found the love of God in Jesus as a Hero Husband.

position of victory, married to the greatest conqueror in human history. While men have conquered nations and one another, Jesus, our Husband, has conquered hell, death, and the grave only to hand that victory over to us and make us more than conquerors. So many live their lives looking for true love, only to have lived life alone. But the Christian has found the love of God in Jesus as a Hero Husband. What a magnanimous Husband we have in Jesus. Welcome to our union in Christ!

ABOUT DUANE SHERIFF

Duane Sheriff is the Senior and Founding Pastor of Victory Life Church, a multi-campus church which is headquartered in Durant, Oklahoma. Pastor Duane travels the world speaking at conferences, churches, as well as Charis Bible Colleges. He has a passion to see people discover who they are meant to be and grow in their relationship with Jesus. His first book, *Identity Theft*, was released in 2017. Pastor Duane and his wife, Sue, have 4 children and 10 grandchildren.

For free teachings by Pastor Duane Sheriff,
visit his website at www.pastorduane.com

The Harrison House Vision

Proclaiming the truth and the power

of the Gospel of Jesus Christ with excellence.

Challenging Christians

to live victoriously,

grow spiritually,

know God intimately.

Connect with us on
Facebook @ HarrisonHousePublishers
and Instagram @ HarrisonHousePublishing
so you can stay up to date with news
about our books and our authors.

Visit us at **www.harrisonhouse.com**
for a complete product listing as well as
monthly specials for wholesale distribution.

Printed in Great Britain
by Amazon

81055255R00147